**Creative
Math/Art Activities
for the Primary Grades**

Creative
Math/Art Activities
for the Primary Grades

Sonia Daleki Forseth, Ph.D.
Associate Professor
University of South Florida
St. Petersburg Campus

Prentice-Hall, Inc.
Englewood Cliffs, New Jersey

Prentice-Hall International, Inc., *London*
Prentice-Hall of Australia, Pty. Ltd., *Sydney*
Prentice-Hall Canada Inc., *Toronto*
Prentice-Hall of India Private Ltd., *New Delhi*
Prentice-Hall of Japan, Inc., *Tokyo*
Prentice-Hall of Southeast Asia Pte. Ltd., *Singapore*
Whitehall Books, Ltd., *Wellington, New Zealand*
Editora Prentice-Hall do Brasil Ltda., *Rio de Janeiro*

Library of Congress Cataloging in Publication Data

Forseth, Sonia Daleki
    Creative math/art activities for the primary grades.

    Includes index.
    1. Mathematics—Study and teaching (Primary)
    2. Creative activities and seat work. I. Title.
    QA135.5.F627 1984   372.7   83-26918

ISBN 0-13-190109-5

Printed in the United States of America

ABOUT THE AUTHOR

Sonia Daleki Forseth, Ph.D., is Associate Professor in the Early Childhood/Reading/Language Arts Department at the University of South Florida, where she supervises interns in the Teacher Training program and teaches Methods courses. Her doctoral thesis at the University of Minnesota was based on her work showing how the core mathematics curriculum can be enhanced by using the visual arts and the natural creative ability of teachers and children.

For the past eighteen years Dr. Forseth has conducted many seminars and workshops throughout the country on the coordination of mathematics and the creative arts in elementary and secondary classrooms. She has also written articles for numerous professional journals, designed eight Math/Art posters, and is co-author of twenty-four books, eight posters, and several booklets for *Project MINNEMAST*, with which she began her career as writer and illustrator of children's stories and creative lessons. Her most recent publications, available from Developmental Learning Materials, are four posters and a teacher's manual on "Colors and Patterns" for preK-3 teachers.

ABOUT THIS RESOURCE

The purpose of this math/art activities book is to help you, the primary grade teacher, channel your students' natural creativity into learning mathematics. It includes more than 200 stimulating, ready-to-use activities to develop children's thinking skills through concrete experiences that combine visual self-expression and mathematical concepts. All of these activities explore basic concepts taught in the mathematics curriculum from kindergarten through Grade 3.

For easy use, the book is organized into 12 sections corresponding to the areas covered in many core primary mathematics curricula:

1. Mathematics Readiness
2. Counting
3. Numeration
4. Basic Skills
5. Place Value
6. Simple Fractions
7. Measurement
8. Geometry
9. Symmetry and Patterns
10. Money
11. Time
12. Creative Problem Solving

Each section focuses on a number of major concepts in the particular mathematics area. It presents a series of objectives relating to each concept, followed by one or more activities to help children achieve the stated competencies. To ensure its successful use, every activity provides a complete list of materials needed and step-by-step directions for carrying it out. Many graphic illustrations accompany the activities. Some offer student worksheet material that can be photostated just as it is for immediate classroom use with individual students, small groups, or the entire class.

Creative Math/Art Activities for the Primary Grades is designed as a complete "enrichment package" to supplement your regular mathematics program. All of the activities were carefully selected to reinforce children's learning through actual manipulation of materials commonly found in the primary classroom. They give children practice in ordering and classifying as they use art materials and apply mathematics principles to creative situations.

You will find that many of the activities both challenge the gifted child and provide successful experiences for the slow learner. Some explore geometric concepts while also giving children opportunities to apply symmetry principles; these will help prepare children to learn higher-order geometric principles in the later grades. The activities for reinforcing basic skills are unique and motivating in that they present students with a fresh approach to learning basic operations.

The book will also be a useful source of problem-solving experiences for your students. Many of the activities are structured to give children situations to which they can apply their own creative ideas and produce their own unique, yet realistic and practical, solutions. Thus their products are the results of their own thinking and problem-solving skills.

Creative Math/Art Activities will help the teacher and students realize that learning mathematics can be a rewarding, enriching, and creative experience. The activities will add a new dimension to virtually any math curriculum and may be used to reinforce regular lessons or to provide enrichment activity just for fun. The teacher can choose an activity in which the whole class can participate or one that meets the needs of individual children. And, since directions and materials for each activity are clearly stated, many of the activities easily can be adapted for use in a learning center where students work independently.

However you decide to use this book remember that children's imaginations are precious. Let them express their own ideas, and remember that their creative work is sacred to them. Display their creations in your classroom. Children will take pride in their accomplishments, and this display will give them a fine success experience in the mathematics class.

Sonia Daleki Forseth

ACKNOWLEDGMENTS

I wish to thank Connie McFarland, my student, for her help, as well as Pam Salvatori, Vicki Bowden and Mary Ann Harrell, who typed the manuscript. Thanks also to Donna Cerrone and Sherra Buys for their help in organizing the Skills Index.

I would also like to acknowledge Rita Damon of High Point Elementary School in Clearwater, Florida, and Carol Salfa of the American Overseas School in Rome, Italy, for their valuable ideas and suggestions.

Contents

Section 1

MATHEMATICS READINESS

To the teacher

This section begins with activities that develop three readiness concepts that refer to opposites: long and short, large and small, and thin and thick. Children need to know the differences between these concepts, which are often attributes found in objects being compared. By learning these differences, children are able to classify their ideas and to store knowledge, which will later help them sort out various ideas and help them to think logically. The art activities in this section provide the child with an opportunity to show if he or she has actually grasped the difference between long and short, thick and thin, or large and small.

It is important to encourage children to talk about their creative work. For example, showing and telling about the large clown and the small clown in a picture will verbally reinforce these concepts that are needed to think in the language of mathematics.

The next part of the section provides a series of creative activities which reinforce children's understanding of basic shapes: circles, triangles, squares, and diamonds or rectangles. Helping children become sensitive to basic shapes enables them to express their impressions and feelings about the world around them. They are encouraged to identify basic shapes to help them represent the objects in their creative work. Shape in mathematics thus becomes another property of an object. Being able to identify these shapes aids children in organizing information. This in turn introduces them to the world of geometry.

The last part of the section includes a set of creative activities which help children learn the differences between spatial directions, such as above and below, and left and right. It is important for children to have an awareness of their environment, that is, an awareness of where they exist and stand in space. In the kindergarten and early primary grades, they are beginning to represent this spatial concept in their creative visual work. They begin to develop a sense of feeling for the ground (below) and the sky (above). Often this is indicated as the base line or ground line at the bottom of a drawing or a run of blue for the sky across the top of a drawing paper.

These concepts—up and down, left and right—are important in mathematics. They become a way of ordering the world in which children live and defining children's spatial relationships to things and objects existing in that world. A very good introduction to some of the research on how children react to the space in which they live is *The Child's Conception of Space*, by Jean Piaget and Barbel Inhelder.

Children at the primary level have specific characteristics that must be considered by the teacher. Many primary grade children have a short interest span. Do not take too much time for any activity. Fifteen minutes usually are sufficient. Children at this age tend to be self-centered and need approval of what they do. Compliment and encourage them as often as possible. Display their work, too. Children like to draw about what they feel and what they know. Their drawings will provide information to you about what individual children have achieved in mathematics. They will use color imaginatively, and they will make important things large. Your sensitivity to children's characteristics will help to make these creative activities a very pleasant way of experiencing and learning the language of mathematics.

CONCEPT: Recognizing and Naming Opposites— Thin and Thick

MOBILE-LOONIES

Materials: Variety of balloons
String
Magic marker

Procedure:

1. Give each child three or four balloons. Have the children decorate the deflated balloons with magic markers. These balloons are flat and thin.

2. The balloons may be difficult to knot at the ends. Instruct the child to blow up the balloon and, while he has the balloon in his mouth, have him tie a string around the end as tight as he can. You may also help in this procedure.

3. Have each child blow up three or four balloons. Discuss the difference between the thin deflated balloon and the thick inflated balloon.

4. Make a mobile-loonie by tying together the three or four balloons. Then hang each mobile-loonie from the ceiling.

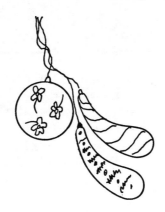

THE THIN AND FAT BOOK

Materials: one sheet of white drawing paper 12-by-18 inches
two sheets of 12-by-18-inch newsprint
scissors, glue, crayons
Sunday comic section
Various macaroni and spaghetti pieces

Procedure:

1. The children will make three individual pages for their thin and thick book.

2. The first page will be on a 12-by-18-inch sheet of newsprint. Tell the children to fold the paper in half.

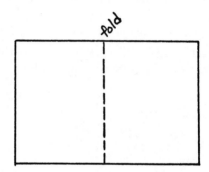

On the left side of the fold, tell them to draw a thin bird, a thin cookie, or a thin ice-cream cone. On the right side of the fold, tell them to draw a fat, thick bird, or a fat, thick cookie, or a fat, thick ice-cream cone.

3. The second page will be a repeat of the first. Fold the page in half and instruct the children to find a picture of a thin person from the Sunday comic section. Glue it onto the left side of the fold. Then have them find a picture of a heavier, thicker person and glue it onto the right side. Instruct the child to draw a friend for each person—a thin friend for this thin comic-strip find and a fat, thick friend for the fat, thick comic-strip find.

4. The cover of the book will be made on the sheet of construction paper. Have the children fold the paper in half. On the left side of the fold, have them make a design by gluing thin spaghetti or macaroni. On the right side, have the children make a design using only thick macaroni and spaghetti.

5. Staple the whole book together.

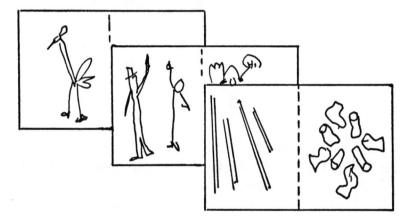

This activity reinforces the concepts of thin and thick, right and left.

CONCEPT: Recognizing and Naming Opposites—
Large and Small

LETTER-HEAD PEOPLE

Materials: Magazines
   Newspapers
   Scissors
   Glue
   Two sheets of construction paper

Procedure:

1. On one day, have the children cut out a set of large letters and a set of small letters from a magazine. Two of each should be sufficient.

2. On the second day, have the children cut out two large faces and two small faces from a magazine.

3. Instruct the children to design a letter-head person. Match up a large head with a large letter. Glue it onto a sheet of paper. The letter becomes the body. Arms and legs may be other letters or the children may wish to draw them into the figure.

4. Repeat the procedure for a small letter-head person. Glue a small head onto a small letter.

   This activity may be extended into a language arts activity. Ask the children if they know the name of the letter they used for the body.

YUM YUM PLATES

Materials: Large paper plates
Small paper plates
Magazines
Crayons
Scissors
Glue

Procedure:

1. Give each child one large or one small paper plate.
2. Instruct the child to find large pictures of food to glue on the large plate and small food to glue pictures of small food on the small plate.
3. On a bulletin board have a large area representing a large table and a small area representing a small table on the bulletin board. Have the children place the large plates of food on the large table and the small plates of food on the small table.

CONCEPT: Recognizing and Naming Opposites— Long and Short

FOREST FROLICS

Materials: Long and short leaves; grasses collected from outdoors
Small bags
Glue
White drawing paper, 12-by-18 inches
Crayons

Procedure:

1. While supervising the children outdoors, collect long and short leaves, grasses, and twigs and place findings into bags.

2. Indoors, give each child a sheet of construction paper. Fold it in half. The left side of the fold is for long things and the right side of the fold is for short things.

3. Instruct the children to draw a ground line on their papers.

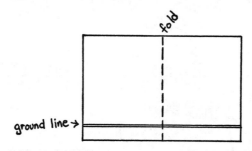

4. Tell the children they are going to make a forest. Have them glue all the long twigs, grasses, and leaves on the left side. Then have them glue all the short grasses, twigs, and leaves on the right side. They may wish to add animals by drawing them in with crayon. If you feel the paper is too small for the activity, use one sheet for short things and a second sheet for long things. Instruct the children to draw the base line.

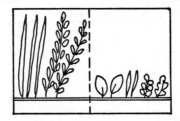

This activity reinforces long, short, right, left, and base line.

HAIRY-DOS

Materials: White glue
Crayons
Various sizes of macaroni and spaghetti
Two 9-by-12 inch white drawing paper for each child

Procedure:

1. Give each child two sheets of white construction paper. Have them draw a large circle on each piece.

2. One sheet will be for long things only; the other for short things only.

3. On the "long" sheet, have the children draw long eyes, nose, and mouth. Then tell them to create a hairdo for the long face using long spaghetti. Glue the spaghetti onto the sheet.

4. On the "short" sheet, have the children draw short eyes, nose, and mouth and glue on short pieces of macaroni.

MAKING A CHAIN

Materials: Strips of multicolored construction paper cut into 1-by-12 inches
Glue

Procedure:

1. During the first fifteen minutes, have each child make a paper chain.

2. After fifteen minutes, instruct the children to stop where they are in their work.
3. Randomly hang each chain from a peg or pin on the bulletin board.
4. Then have the children rank-order each child's chain length by ordering them from shortest to longest on the bulletin board.

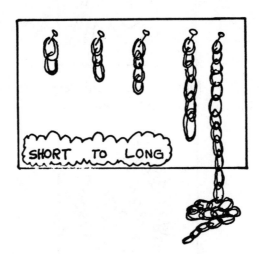

5. Finally, make the longest chain by connecting all the pieces together.

CONCEPT: Recognizing and Naming Geometric Shapes— Circles

CIRCLE McGIRCLES

Materials: Circular pie plates
Crayons
Paste
Various-sized precut color construction paper circles
Straws
Stapler

Procedure:

1. For motivation, tell the children they are each going to make a pretend lollipop called Circle McGircle.

2. Instruct the children to design their lollipop using various circles as decorations. These colored circles can be glued onto the pie plate. They may wish to use crayons to further decorate their creation.

3. The handle of the Circle McGircle is a straw which is stapled to the pie plate.

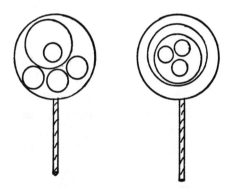

4. You may wish to follow-up the activity by having the children describe their lollipops. What colors did they use? Which circles are large? Which circles are small? All of the Circle McGircles could be displayed on the bulletin board by arranging them in a circular pattern.

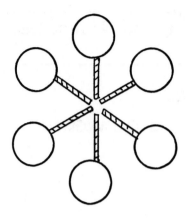

PURPLE CIRCLE BURPLE PRINTS

Materials: A found object that is circular
Tempera paint (purple)
Brush
Newsprint

Procedure:

1. Motivate the children by telling them that they are going to make Purple Circle Burples. Have each child select a circular object, such as a jar cover, an onion sliced in half, or a soft sponge cut into a circular shape. Sponges work very well for this activity.

2. Have pie pans with colors of purple tempera paint and brushes available. Instruct the children to lightly coat the surface of the circular object with a thin layer of paint.

3. Press the object onto a sheet of newsprint in order to make a print. Encourage the children to make a sheet full of circular patterns.

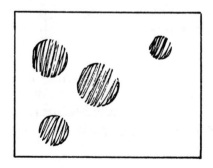

4. After the prints are made, ask the children to count how many Purple Circle Burples they placed on their papers. Can they write the appropriate number on the papers?

5. Display all of the Purple Circle Burples on the bulletin board.

This activity provides the children with experience in printmaking, identifying circular objects, the color purple, and assigning the proper number to the objects used in the experience.

CONCEPT: Recognizing and Naming Geometric Shapes— Triangles

TRI-PLANES

Materials: Precut white construction paper triangles
Crayons
String

Procedure:

1. Give each child a large precut equilateral triangle.

2. Tell the children to decorate the triangle any way they wish. Decorate both surfaces, front and back.

3. Have the children fold their triangles to make paper airplanes.

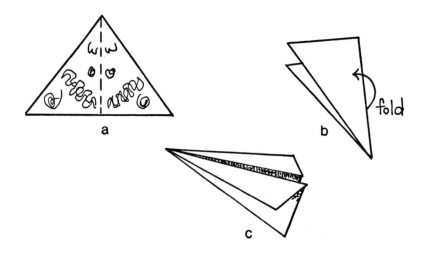

4. Hang up the tri-plane from the ceiling. Discuss all the triangle shapes that can be found in the tri-plane after all the folds are made. This may be a little difficult, but it helps reinforce perception of triangular regions.

TILLIE TRIANGLES

Materials: Construction paper
Scissors
Glue or paste

Procedure:

1. Precut various sizes and colors of triangles for the children.
2. Tell them they are going to make some Tillie Triangles, which are really silly triangles.
3. Have the children group various triangles together until they feel they are making a Tillie Triangle monster.
4. Glue down the shapes.

5. Help the children describe their pictures by having them think up basic sentences about their pictures. Follow the noun-verb kernel sentence pattern; for example

    The dragon jumps.
    The monster smiles.
    The triangle runs.

This activity reinforces the identification of triangular shapes and introduces the child to thinking of a basic sentence.

CONCEPT: Recognizing and Naming Geometric Shapes— Squares

SQUARE MOSAICS

Materials: Various-sized squares cut from construction paper—
1-, 2-, 3-, 4-, 5-, and 6-inch squares
Glue
One 8-inch construction paper square for each child

Procedure:

1. Motivate the children by telling them they are going to make a large mosaic mural that will decorate the wall.

2. Give each child one 8-inch square cut from construction paper. Have an assortment of smaller squares in piles available from which the children may choose what they prefer.

3. Instruct them to glue various sizes of squares onto their large square piece and make one decorated mosaic tile. Encourage overlapping and repetition.

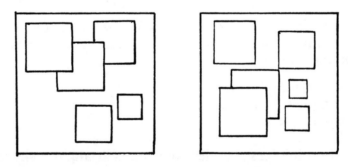

4. When the children are finished, tape each square side by side onto a wall until a large region is covered. This makes an excellent environmental decoration in the classroom.

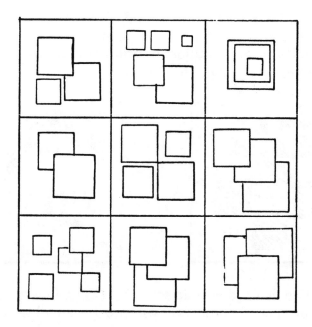

Retain the basic square shape by taping each mosaic in an equal array of rows and columns. Reinforce color recognition by asking a child to point to a small blue square or a large yellow square.

SQUARE PRINTS

Materials: Gum eraser (end)
Print pad
Newsprint (9-by-12 inches)

Procedure:

1. Give each child a section of a gum eraser. One eraser sliced in half works well.

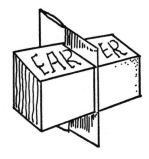

2. Have each child cover the square end of the eraser with printer's ink by pressing it into a print pad and then stamping it onto a sheet of newsprint. Have various colors of printing pads available.

3. Ask the children to make a design using only squares and various colors from the print pad.

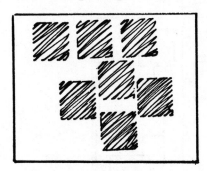 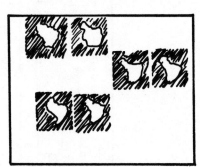

4. For variation, have each child scratch a design into the end of the eraser with a sharp pencil point. This will provide an added dimension to the pattern.

CONCEPT: Recognizing and Naming Other Geometric Shapes

SHAPE SCULPTURES

Materials: One (or more) small cardboard box
Old magazines
Glue
Scissors
Construction paper
Clear tape (or masking tape)

Procedure:

1. Find a small cardboard box and seal it shut with some clear tape or masking tape.

2. The box will either be a cube or a rectangle in shape. The box has six sides. On each side, decide on a shape that you will use to cover the side by searching through magazines for that shape and gluing it to the box. For example, one side might be covered with only square shapes that you find in pictures from a magazine. The other side may be covered with circular shapes, a third side with triangular shapes, a fourth side with rectangular shapes, and a fifth side with a combination of shapes.

3. Cut or print the word SHAPES from construction paper. Have the children glue their shapes to a sheet of construction paper and glue that to one side of the box.

4. When you have finished, share your box with a friend and display them. If everyone makes a box, make a huge box sculpture by piling them up as if they were blocks. They are very sturdy so allow the children to arrange and rearrange them as they wish.

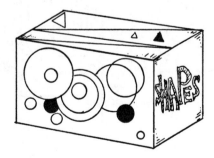

5. A variation would be to cover one side with pictures of red objects only, another side with pictures of green objects only, and the remaining sides with pictures of yellow, blue, purple, and black objects.

RECTANGLE SCULPTURES

Materials: Rectangular-shaped boxes
White glue

Procedure:

1. Instruct the children to search for cardboard boxes at home that are rectangular in shape. They might bring in two or three tissue or cereal boxes.

2. Have the children glue their boxes together in any way they like.

3. After their boxes dry securely, have everyone come together and glue all their boxes together in order to form a large class sculpture.

4. Display the rectangular box sculpture.

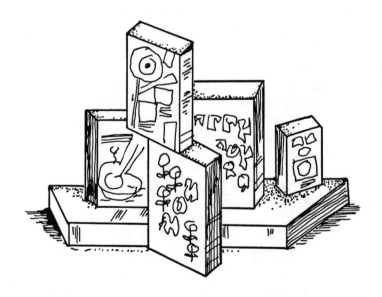

MAGIC RECTANGLES

Materials: Three straws for each child

One 12-by-18 inch sheet of construction paper

Glue

Scissors

Crayons

Procedure:

1. Tell the children they will make a rectangle from three straws.

2. Instruct the children to cut one of their three straws in half.

3. Then instruct the children to glue the straws into a rectangular shape. Tell them the straws make a little window.

4. Tell the children to pretend that the window is magic and that they can see anything they want to see. Have them illustrate what they see happening inside the window and outside the window.

This activity reinforces the concept of inside, outside, and rectangular shapes.

CONCEPT: Understanding Spatial Relationships—
Above and Below

SEA AND SKY

Materials: Crayons
White drawing paper

Procedure:

1. Have each child fold a sheet of drawing paper in half lengthwise.

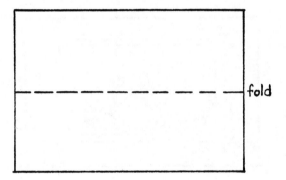

2. Instruct the children to draw a line with a dark crayon on the fold line. Then tell them that line is a line dividing the sea from the sky.

3. Ask the children to draw pictures of things they might find in the sky above the line.

4. Then ask the children to draw pictures of things they would find in the sea, below the line.

THE LIVING THINGS MURAL

Materials: Paper   Found objects
Scissors   Paint
Glue   Brushes
Magazines

Procedure:

1. Cover a bulletin board with white paper. Draw a horizontal line along the center of the paper.

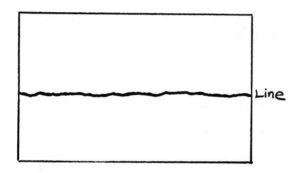

2. Have the children make a class mural by drawing and gluing pictures of all the things they can think of and find that represent the following:

   a. All the things that live above the ground.
   b. All the things that live below the ground.

CONCEPT: Understanding Spatial Relationships— Left and Right

COLOR COLLAGE COLLECTION

Materials: Magazines
Scissors
Glue
White 12-by-18-inch construction paper
Crayons

Procedure:

1. Fold the drawing paper in half. Draw a line down the fold line.

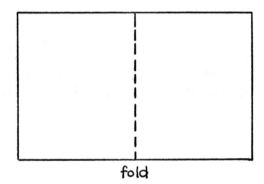

fold

2. On the left side of the line, paste all the blue pictures a child can find.

3. On the right side of the line, paste all the red things a child can find.

4. Have the children do this for each of the following color combinations:

Orange and purple
Green and yellow
Black and pink

DRAWINGS OF ME

Materials: Newsprint (12-by-18 inches)
Crayons

Procedure:

1. Give the children two sheets of newsprint each. Instruct them to fold them in half.

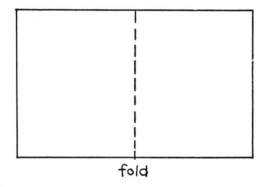

fold

2. On one sheet of the paper, have the child trace the left hand to the left of the fold line, then the right hand to the right of the fold line.

3. Repeat this with the feet on another sheet of newsprint. Have the child remove his or her shoes and trace the left foot on the left of the fold line and the right foot to the right of the fold line.

4. Then instruct the child to take the tracing of his or her hands and do the following:

   a. On the right hand, draw a picture of a square.
   b. On the left hand, put a large red circle which can be colored.

Then take the tracing of the feet. Instruct the children to the following:

   a. On the right foot, draw a stocking.
   b. On the left foot, draw a shoe.

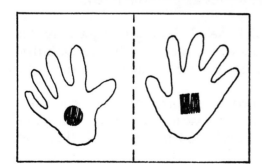   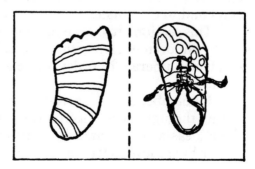

This activity reinforces following directions, right and left, and identification of shapes.

Section 2
COUNTING

To the teacher

The series of activities in this section revolve around counting and sequencing numbers. All of the activities can be adjusted to meet the needs of the children.

The simplest or easiest activities emphasize counting orally from zero to ten. Since zero (0) is a symbol and a place marker, it may be confused as representing the empty set. It is suggested that the children should not make a creative product using that symbol. This may confuse them. However, you may want to indicate the empty set by a creative project void of any elaboration or use of materials. In the chain-making activity, encourage the children to write the numerals as high as they are able.

Sequencing numerals and counting will become more meaningful to the child if you provide as many verbal opportunities as possible to count to the class and to classmates.

This section provides many ideas in which the whole class may participate. As the children work together in a group, they will reinforce each other's ability to place numerals in order and encourage each other to count into the high numbers.

Remember that the activities are designed to reinforce the child's counting ability through the use of creative experience. It is wise to allow them to develop their ideas as freely and as creatively as possible. Try not to inhibit them by prescribing the activity down to the last detail. For example, in chain-making, if some children wish to decorate their chains with crayon patterns or cut out construction paper objects and glue them onto a link, allow them to do so. Each set a child makes should be a reflection of his or her personality and ideas. Don't allow the activities to become "busy work" for the children. Try to use the activities as both a learning experience in counting and a creative experience. This can be achieved by developing in the children a feeling of self-confidence in ideas, manipulating of materials, and ability to demonstrate counting.

CONCEPT: Counting Orally from 0 to 10

NUMBER SPOONS

Materials: Wooden dixie cup spoons (ten for each child)
Magic marker pens—various colors
Glue
Yarn pieces
Small beans
Pipe cleaners

Procedure:

1. Give each child a set of ten wooden dixie cup spoons.

2. Instruct them to decorate each spoon by drawing a face on each and decorating it so it resembles a small person.

3. Have the children line up the spoons from left to right and count orally in a sequence as they do so. These spoons can be used as puppets for storytelling.

SHOE BOX FLOATS PARADE

Materials: Old shoe boxes (one for each child)
Assorted papers (tissue, construction, crepe)
Assorted decorations (beads, seeds, buttons)
Scissors

Procedure:

1. Have the children bring in old shoe boxes and have each child decorate them using a theme. Tell the children they will be designing a float for a parade, and they can use any materials they wish to decorate the shoe box.

2. Assign a numeral zero to ten to each shoe box. The numeral depends on how many sets of ten children are in the class. Have the children order their floats in proper sequence for the parade. Some classes may have two sets of numerals zero to ten.

3. Use the parade of floats as a number line for addition and subtraction problems.

CONCEPT: Counting Orally from 0 to 100

THE SCHOOL OF FISH

Materials: 100 sheets of white construction paper, 12-by-18 inches
Tempera paint
Scissors
String

Procedure:

1. Instruct the child to paint a large fish on the sheet of construction paper.

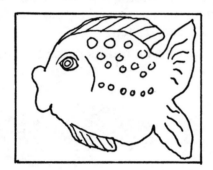

2. Cut out the fish and turn it over. Paint another fish on the back side so that both sides are covered with paint. If you do not want to use tempera paint, crayons will do.

3. Attach a string to the fish and hang 100 fish from the ceiling.

4. Have the children make exactly 100 fish and orally keep track of how many are completed.

CONCEPT: Recognizing and Writing Numbers Up to 100

MAKING A CHAIN

Materials: Scissors
Construction paper
White glue
Ruler
Crayon
Stapler

Procedure:

1. Cut construction paper into strips about 1 inch wide and 12 inches long.

2. On each strip of paper, number the strips from 1 to 100. If more than one child is making a chain, instruct the children to number the strips sequentially so that a number is not repeated.

3. Make a chain by dabbing white glue on one end of each strip. Make a loop and stick together. Interlock each loop before gluing ends together.

4. Use many colors to make the chain. Perhaps a group can make the "longest chain in the world!" Hang it on the ceiling. How many links does the class chain have? Encourage the children to write larger numbers beyond 100. This project could turn into a school project and the numbers may go into the hundreds.

THE SOCCER T's

Materials: 100 sheets of white construction paper
100 T-shirts precut for each sheet of construction paper
Glue
Crayons

Procedure:

1. Give each child a precut T-shirt.

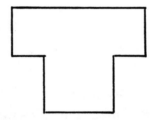

2. Tell each child to draw a man or a woman to fill in the T-shirt. First instruct them to glue it onto a sheet of construction paper, then to draw the man or woman. You may wish to have the T-shirt predittoed onto the white construction paper.
3. Next have each child write a different numeral from 1 to 100 on the T-shirt.
4. Order the people in proper sequence around the room.

CONCEPT: Counting Orally to 500

STAR INVADERS

Materials: Two boxes of gummed stars (multicolor)
White drawing paper
Crayons
Scissors

Procedure:

1. Cover a bulletin board with dark blue construction paper.
2. Have the child stick on 500 gummed stars in order to create a galaxy.
3. Encourage the child to count orally.
4. A follow-up creative activity would be to have the children paint some planets and other children design creatures from Star Invaders that live on these planets.

A HEADSTART ON NUMBERS

Materials: Magazines
Scissors
Glue

Procedure:

1. Draw a large silhouette of a head on white paper 4-by-3 feet.

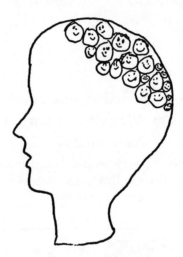

2. Have the children cut out 500 pictures of people's heads and fill in the outline with heads. Assign some children to keep track of how many heads have been cut by counting and sorting the pictures into five boxes of 100 each.

CONCEPT: Counting by 2's to 20

NOAH'S ARK

Materials: Construction paper in various colors
Scissors
Crayons

Procedure:

1. On the bulletin board, place a large ark with a plank.

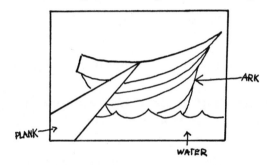

2. Tell the child to draw a pair of animals, mamas and papas, and place them one by one boarding the ark and in the ark.

3. Count the animals by 2's.

CONCEPT: Counting by 5's to 100

GIVE ME FIVE

Materials: A pair of clear plastic food gloves for each child
Rubber cement
Colored feathers (Old feather dusters are good for this.)
Yarn
Beads
Beans
Magic markers

Procedure:

1. Give each child a pair of gloves, some rubber cement, a few feathers, and other paraphernalia.

2. Instruct the children to make a finger puppet on each finger. Some children may use the whole glove for the puppet face.

3. Line up the children and have them count by 5's to 100 by holding up their puppet when it is their turn.

HANDY-MAN SPECIAL

Materials: Plastic gloves
Rolls of colored toilet tissue
Yarn

Procedure:

1. On bulletin board, make a clown with ten arms.

2. Instruct the children to stuff plastic gloves with colored toilet tissue and tie up the end. Make twenty hands.

3. Attach two pairs to each arm and have each child count to 100 by 5's.
4. The hands can be labeled by 5's.

CONCEPT: Counting by 10's to 100

10 BY 10's

Materials: Tissue paper
Pipe cleaners
Glue
String
Construction paper

Procedure:

1. *Flowers*—Make ten flowers for one bouquet. Use pipe cleaners, tissue paper, and string to make the flowers. Cut the tissue paper into rectangles, and tie the sheets of multi-color tissue with string. Wrap a pipe cleaner around the tissue flower for a stem. Bind together in bunches and display in a vase.

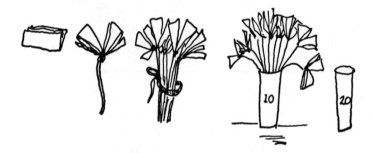

2. *Train*—Make a train of ten boxcars and have the children place ten objects in each. The objects can be drawn on paper and cut out. Glue them onto the boxes.

CIRCUS TENT

Materials: Yarn for circus ring
Drawing paper
Scissors
Crayons

Procedure:

1. On a bulletin board, place ten circus rings large enough to hold ten objects.
2. Instruct the children to illustrate one of the following in each ring:

   ten lions
   ten clowns
   ten dogs
   ten elephants
   ten acrobats
   ten tigers
   ten bands
   ten bears
   ten horses
   ten jugglers

Section 3
NUMERATION

To the teacher

The activities in this section utilize regular classroom supplies such as construction paper, scissors, glue, and other simple art materials. Each activity can be produced by the children with very little teacher preparation. Allow the children to design and make the images for bulletin boards, make up their own worksheets and games, and display their work in a manner they think is appealing.

The numeration objectives include working with numbers 0 to 100, identifying numbers one less and one greater up to 100, recognizing symbols >, <, and =, and an introduction to negative numbers.

The classification lessons provide the children with an opportunity to reinforce logical thinking patterns. The lesson on identifying odd and even numbers includes three reproducible worksheets for the children.

CONCEPT: Identifying the Numerals from 0 to 10

NUMBER HATS

Materials: Multicolored tissue paper precut into circles approximately
6-by-8 inches
Yarn (12 inches long), two per child
Construction paper, 12-by-18 inches
Glue
Stapler

Procedure:

1. Give each child four to ten separate sheets of tissue paper that have been precut into circles.

2. Have the children gather the center of one sheet to make a bow shape. Squeeze the gathered region and twist once.

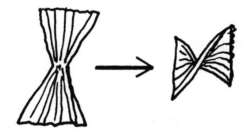

3. Instruct each child to make multicolored bows with which to decorate his or her hat. Glue the bows onto the sheet of 12-by-18 inch construction paper. Write the number on the sheet of construction paper that represents the number of bows glued onto the hat.

4. Staple the two ends of the construction paper together in order to form a cone. Attach yarn pieces by stapling the yarn onto the paper for ties on the hat.

5. Have the children line up in proper numeral sequence of 1 to 10.

BIGGER BUGS

Materials: Construction paper
              Crayons
              Scissors

Procedure:

1. Each child makes a set of bugs that increase in size from construction paper. Each bug is cut a little larger than the one before it.
2. Label Bug 1 through 10 from smallest to largest.

3. Have children arrange bugs from smallest to largest. This should help the child order the numbers in proper sequence because the larger the number the larger the bug.

SAND PAINTINGS

Materials: Cornmeal, rice, or white sand
White glue
Crayons
Vegetable coloring (red, yellow, blue, green)
Heavy paper (tagboard) 9-by-12 inches

Procedure:

1. The night before using the cornmeal, rice, or white sand, place one cup of each ingredient into plastic or tin containers. Sprinkle a few drops of vegetable coloring into the contents of the containers and stir until rice or cornmeal is colored. Make as many different colors as you wish (e.g., red, yellow, blue, green, purple). Brown can be obtained from instant coffee or tea.

2. Instruct the children to draw, using a crayon, any number of objects on the piece of tagboard. You should specify the total number than can be drawn; for instance, 1 up to 10, etc.

3. Have the children outline their design and fill in a portion of their design using white glue. Then have the children drop the colored rice or cornmeal into the area that has been covered by the glue, shaking the loose grains of rice or cornmeal back into the proper color container.

4. When the sand painting is completed, have the children assign the proper numeral for the number of objects in their illustration.

CONCEPT: Matching Objects on a One-to-One Basis

THE FROGS AND THE BUGS

Materials: Lima beans, navy beans, green peas
White glue
Yarn (ten for each child)
Tape
Two egg cartons

Procedure:

1. Instruct the children to make a batch of frogs and bugs by gluing the beans together as shown.

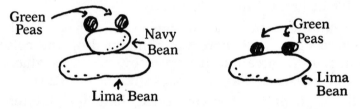

Frogs   *Bugs*

2. Place one frog in one egg holder in an egg carton, then two frogs in another egg holder, then three frogs in another egg holder. Continue until ten frogs are in one holder.

3. In a second egg carton, place the bugs, one in one egg holder, two in another egg holder, etc.

4. Tell the children the following story:

    The frogs are hungry for bugs. The bugs are sleeping in the egg pits. Each frog is allowed one bug. Match a frog or a set of frogs with the same amount of bugs by connecting the egg pits with yarn and securing the yarn with tape.

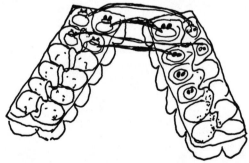

5. Tell the children to make up a frog and bug game.

TEST A FRIEND

Materials: Paper
Pencil
Crayons

Procedure:

1. Tell the children to draw the following objects on a sheet of paper. Do not tell them the number of objects they are to draw. Let them choose.

2. Draw a bunch of bananas.   Draw a school of fish.
Draw a litter of cats.   Draw a herd of cows.
Draw a flock of birds.   Draw a group of children.
Draw a bunch of squares.   Draw a gaggle of geese.

3. Exchange drawings with a friend.

4. Instruct the children to write the correct number of bananas, apples, cats, birds, squares, and fish that were drawn on the paper. Numbers will vary for each set.

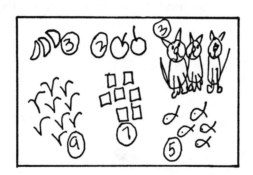

5. Return answer sheet and drawings to the child who originally drew them and have the child check the friend's answers.

CONCEPTS: Recognizing Numbers and Words
from 1 to 20;
Writing Numerals from 1 to 20

"IN THE BAGS"

Materials: Twenty baggies
Large box
Tape
Index cards

Procedure:

1. Put one object in one bag, two in the next, three in next, etc.
2. Place the bags together in a large box.
3. On the chalkboard, write the numerals 1 to 20, but not in order.
4. Have the words one through twenty on index cards.

| NINETEEN | TWO | ELEVEN |

5. Each child picks a baggie from the box. Ask the child to count the objects, find the written numeral on the card for the number of objects in the bag, and tape both under the numeral for the object.

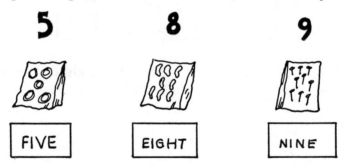

6. When one-to-one correspondence with symbol and written word is completed, have the child sequence the bags and written numerals in proper order.
7. A variation to this activity is to have the children guess and order the bags by feeling how many are in each bag. Then have them check by counting to see if they matched the correct numeral and card with the bag.

NIMBLE NUMERALS

Materials: Paper
Crayons
Cards with number written

Procedure:

1. Instruct the children to make a Nimble Numeral person out of a number symbol. Examples:

2. Display the Nimble Numerals in proper sequence across the chalkboard.
3. Have the children match the written numeral with the proper symbol.

CONCEPT: Ordering Numbers Before and After Certain Numerals from 1 to 20

SUITE DOGS

Materials: Bulletin board
Yarn
Scissors
Construction paper
Crayons

Procedure:

1. Make a Waggy Tail Hotel on the chalkboard or bulletin board.

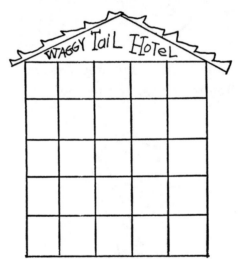

2. Instruct the children to draw a large dog and cut it out. The dog will be used as a guest in the Waggy Tail Hotel. Each dog is given a number to its suite. The suite number is a number written on a tag that is attached to the dog's neck with yarn.

3. As each dog is registered, it is assigned to a suite. Have the child figure out which room in the Hotel the dog is to occupy.

4. You can change the shape of the suites to any arrangement of rows and columns in order to help the children order the dogs in proper sequence.

5. Ask the children which dog comes before a certain suite and which comes after, i.e., does 10 come before or after 9?

SPEEDY SPACE MEN

Materials: Large paper bag
Crayons
Felt-tipped pens

Procedure:

1. Have each child design and make his or her own space helmet out of a paper grocery store bag.

2. Assign a number from 1 to 20 to each child. Make sure the number is on the bag.

3. Ask the children to line up as quickly as Speedy Space Men in proper numerical sequence.

4. Record time each day to see how fast they can do it.

CONCEPT: Ordering Numbers (One More and One Less) Up to 100

LOGIC BINGO

Materials: Construction paper
Scissors
Tape
Pencil
Markers, paints, etc.

Procedure:

1. Give each child a set of numbers up to 100; one child may have 1, 8, 49, and 72; another may have 2, 9, 16, and 44, and so on.

2. Have the child write each number individually on a sheet of paper and decorate it.

3. Call out a number, i.e., 42. Tape that number on the board. Ask the children to tape the number that is one greater than 42 next to it. What number will be one less than 42?

4. Call out another number, i.e., 74. Tape that number on the board. Ask the children to tape up the number that is 8 greater than 72 and 8 less than 72.

5. Call out various numbers with the following variations:
   a. 5 greater than; 5 less than
   b. 10 greater than; 10 less than
   c. 3 greater than; 3 less than
   d. Make up your own sequences
6. Whichever child uses up his or her set of numbers first wins the game.

GREATER KINGS

Materials: Paper
           Print pad

Procedure:

1. Display "greater than" and "less than" symbols.

2. Display the following poem and see if the children can tell you what it means.

   Whom does the arrow point to?
   You are less than me,
   I am greater than you!

3. Make a thumbprint king:

4. King Snoofy's army always had one less man than King Alfred's army. Have the children turn paper lengthwise and draw King Snoofy on the left and King Alfred on the right. On the top of the other side, they should draw the kings again in the opposite order. Draw a line from top to bottom halfway across the page.

KING SNOOFY	KING ALFRED
4	5

KING SNOOFY	KING ALFRED
12	11

5. Instruct the children to put a "greater than" or "less than" sign between the kings.

6. The teacher may call out various numbers between 1 and 100 for either king's army. The children must figure out how many men are in the other king's army and draw a "less than" or "greater than" symbol.

GREAT NUMBERS

Materials: Index cards
Scissors
Construction paper, two sheets of 8 ½-by-11 inches, per child
Pins

Procedure:

1. Tell the children that these are very interesting numbers. They always are greater than their neighbor who is the "little guy" or one less than them.

2. Have each child make an "I'm Great" sign.

3. Assign each child a small card with a number 2 to 25 (or as many numbers as children in the class) and pin it on them. The teacher takes number 1. Let the children take turns finding their neighbor and holding up the "I'm Great" sign.

4. On the following day, continue with the next sequence of numbers (25 to 50). Do this every day until all numbers, 1 to 100, have been assigned.

CONCEPT: Recognizing and Applying Symbols—
Greater Than, Less Than, and Equal To

DRIZZY DRAGON

Materials: Newspaper
Cardboard
Stapler
Paint

Procedure:

1. Give each child two sheets of newspaper. Have the children draw and cut out a side view of a dragon head in duplicate. Tell the children to make sure their dragon has its mouth *wide* open.

2. Staple the edges together leaving an opening where the child will stuff crumpled newspaper. Staple the opening. Have the children paint the dragon head.

3. Tell the children that Drizzy Dragon hates big numbers. Probably big numbers frighten it because it is not as smart as they are. Whenever Drizzy Dragon sees two numbers beside each other, it jumps in the middle and tries to spit fire on the larger number.

   Its mouth is just like the "greater than" and "less than" symbols. The open part is always pointed at the largest number. When the largest number is first, it always says it is "greater than" the other number. When the smaller number is first, it always says it is "less than" the other number.

Drizzy Dragon isn't quite so dumb, though. If it sees some numbers like 5 + 3 _____ 8, it *knows* they are trying to fool it. Neither one is the largest. The numbers 5 + 3 mean the same thing as 8.

You could put numbers on the board and choose children to have their Drizzy Dragon spit fire at the largest number. Instruct the children to read the mathematical sentence using "less than" or "greater than."

Increase in difficulty by using addition facts:

$$1 + 5 \rule{2em}{0.4pt} 8$$
$$1 + 5 \rule{2em}{0.4pt} 6$$
$$1 + 5 \rule{2em}{0.4pt} 4 + 3$$

CONCEPT: Understanding and Recognizing the Need for
Negative Numbers

PIN THE RABBIT ON THE LADDER

Materials: Crayons
Scissors
Bulletin Board
Paper
Tape

Procedure:

1. Each child draws a rabbit eating a carrot. Cut it out.

2. On a bulletin board, example shown in figure, assign a position on the ladder for the rabbit. Can the child find the correct position?

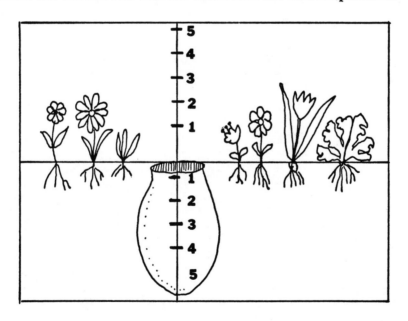

3. Each child traces his or her right and left hand. Cut out each. Assign a positive number and a negative number to each child. Have them write it on the hand.

4. Have each child place his or her hand in the proper sequence on a number line.

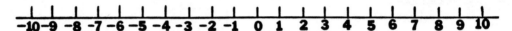

CONCEPT: Identifying Odd and Even Numbers

ODD GAMES FOR EVEN THINKING IDEAS

Materials: Index cards
(optional)

Procedure:

1. Tell the children: 2 – 4 – 6 – 8, who do we appreciate? Do this for the child of the day!

2. Given a number line, X out all the even numbers.

3. Given a number line, put a circle around all the odd numbers.

4. Pair up objects to see if you have an odd or even amount.

5. Cute game: Rules—
   a. Each child has a card that says "odd" on one side and "even" on the other.
   b. Divide the children into two teams. One member from each team stands back to back. They raise a set of fingers in the air when the teacher says, "Go!"

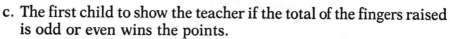

   c. The first child to show the teacher if the total of the fingers raised is odd or even wins the points.

6. Explain that each person has two feet. Therefore, each person needs two shoes. If you have one foot, you need one shoe, but that would be odd (since most people have two feet). If you have two feet, you need a shoe for each foot or two shoes; that would be even. Keep going through this process, five feet would be odd, six feet would be even. Every child would take his or her shoes off and place them in a pile. One child would come before the class and get one shoe. Would it be normal for a child to walk around with only one shoe on? No, so one is an odd number. Would it be normal for a child to walk around with two shoes on? Yes, so two is an even number. Then you bring up another child and go on to three, four, five, etc.

7. Reproduce the following three sheets with Dot-to-Dot connections.

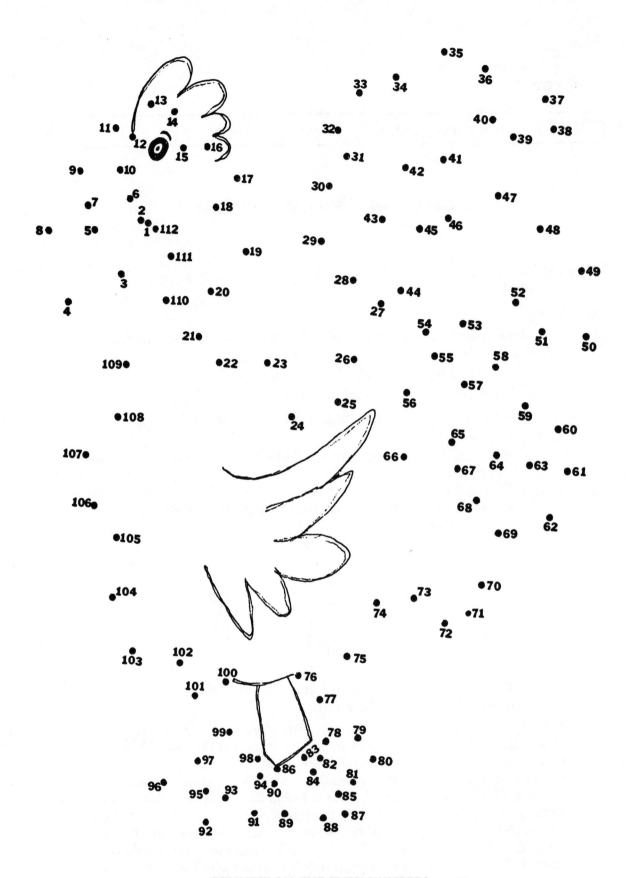

CONNECT ALL THE EVEN NUMBERS.

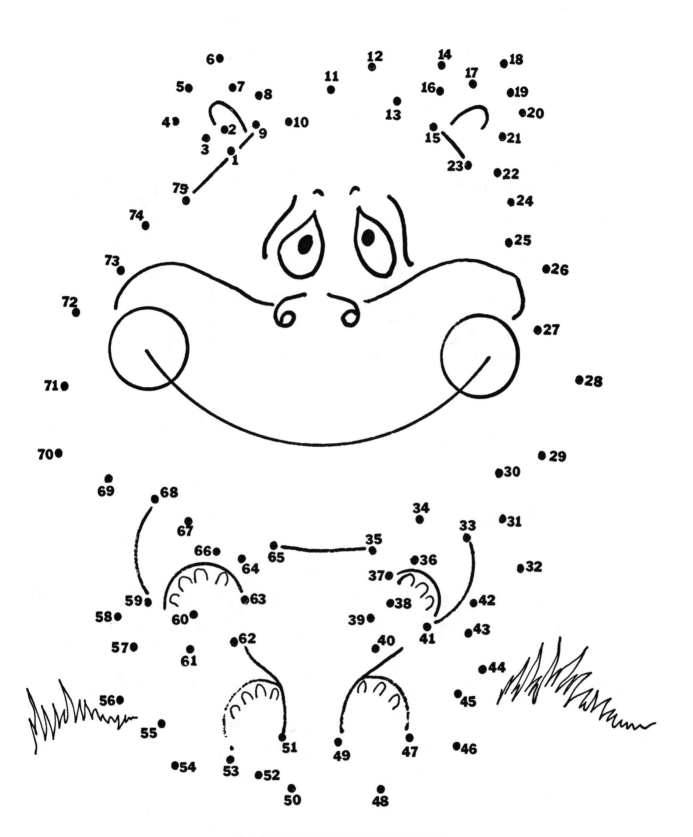

CONNECT ALL THE ODD NUMBERS.

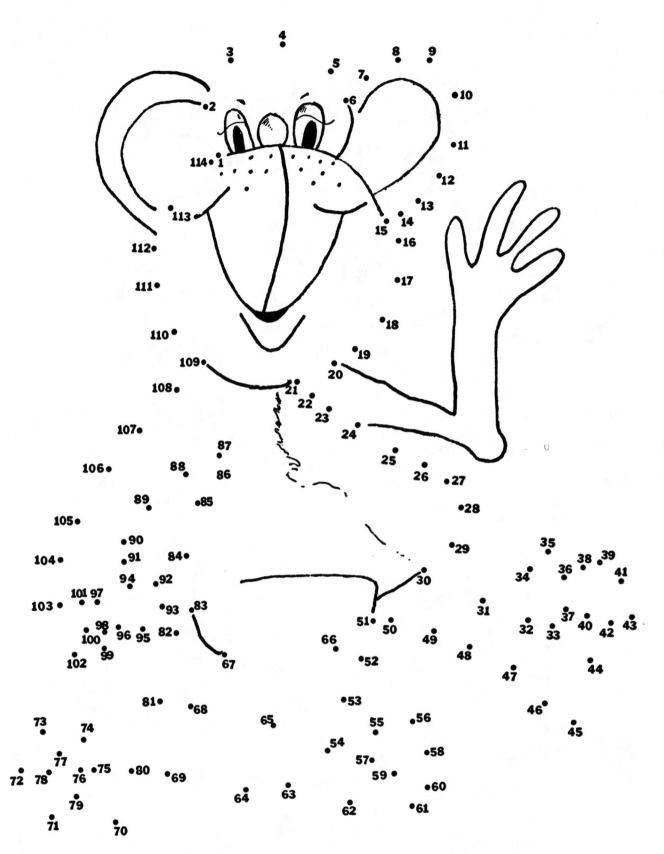

CONNECT ALL THE ODD AND EVEN NUMBERS ON THE MONKEY.

Section 4
BASIC FACTS

To the teacher

When asked what she didn't like about mathematics class, a first grader once responded, "Cut and paste. All we do is cut and paste. I'm sick of cutting and pasting." The following activities focus on basic facts and are designed to guide you away from cutting and pasting activities. Unusual media are suggested in the lessons in order to stimulate the children's imaginations and provide them with creative experiences beyond the cutting and pasting syndrome.

Children need a variety of activities in the mathematics class. If a lesson becomes a set pattern, for example, instruction, paper and pencil task, and a game, some children become numb in their thinking. By varying the media while teaching the basic skills, you will find that the children are developing a new favorable attitude toward the subject.

This section provides children with experiences in learning basic facts while expressing their ideas visually through the manipulation of a variety of materials. Many of the materials needed in these activities can be found at home. The unique set of activities on bookmaking is included and should be given special attention. Forms, images, and motifs often communicate ideas that a child may find difficult to communicate in words. The creative activities enhance the use of symbols in a particular fashion. As words have meaning only in relationship to experiences, so too do creative visual symbols have meaning only in relationship to certain abstract and concrete experiences.

The activities presented here will help children to write and to illustrate their own mathematics books, which in turn reinforces growth in creative visual expression. Encourage the children to build their very own library of mathematical facts. You may want to use the children's work in order to teach other children arithmetic facts.

The specific objectives cover addition and subtraction facts 1 to 10, and then continue on to addition and subtraction facts through 20 with and without regrouping. Multiplication and division are reinforced by suggesting that the children make multiplication array books for various products by factoring various multiplicands.

The instructions for making and binding the basic facts handbook can be found in the Appendix.

CONCEPT: Recognizing Symbols—
Plus (+), Minus (−), and Equal To (=)

MISSING ADDEND RACE

Materials: White drawing paper, 12-by-18 inches
Decorations (cloth, buttons, bottle caps, macaroni, popcorn, beans, glitter)
Scissors
Glue

Procedure:

1. Assign each child a number from 1 through 10.
2. Have the children decorate their numbers using various decorations.

3. Have one child make a "plus sign" and one child make an "equal sign" rather than a number.
4. The teacher will call out two numbers (example: 1 and 6). The largest number will always be the sum.
5. All children with the numbers called should come to the front of the room and stand in the correct position between the plus and the equal signs.
6. The children must then see how quickly they can get everyone with the number of the missing addend in the correct position.
7. You could time this activity and the children could try to "break the record" of previous attempts. The best time of each day could be charted on a bulletin board.

Variation: Do the same thing for subtraction. Give the children some
subtraction problems or have them make up their own.

Example:

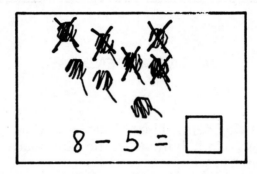

8. Make a book of crayon rubbings showing missing addends for addition.

CONCEPT: Adding Numbers from 1 to 10

FANCY STEP MATH

Materials: Sheet music for "Mary Had a Little Lamb" ("jazzy")

Procedure: Play the song while the students sing the following:

Fancy step a little math, little math, little math,
Fancy step a little math,
Now let's go down the path.

(Spoken) (Chant and walk in a "disco" dance pattern)

1 + 1 is 2 (hey!)
2 + 1 is 3 (hey!)
3 + 1 is 4 (hey!)
4 + 1 is 5 (hey!)

Now we've done a little math, little math, little math,
Now we've done a little math,
Let's try another path.

(Spoken)

5 − 1 is 4 (hey!)
4 − 1 is 3 (hey!)
3 − 1 is 2 (hey!)
2 − 1 is 1 (hey!)
1 − 1 is enough!

Variation: This may also be adapted to multiplication.

BUNNY HOPPERS

Materials: Cotton
Rulers
Adding machine tape
Construction paper
Paper
Paste

Procedure:

1. Motivate the children: tell them they are going to make fluffy rabbits. You may want to make one of your own, which is attached to a stick. This then can be used to demonstrate how the rabbit hops along the number line.

2. Give each child a piece of paper to draw a large rabbit.

3. Have the children cut out the rabbit and paste on cotton balls to make it fluffy.

4. Children can use construction paper to make eyes, nose, and whiskers.

5. Instruct the children on making a mark every six inches on a long piece of adding machine tape. Number each mark from 1 to 10.

6. Have the child sit on the floor in his or her own personal space.

7. Give verbal addition problems and see if children end up on the correct mark.

   Happy hopped two spaces. Then he hopped four spaces. How far did he hop in all? Write on the board: 2 + 4 = _____

   6 + 1 = _____

MAKING NECKLACES

Materials: Straws (colored and cut 1½ or 2 inches long) placed into one box
Construction paper cut into 1-inch squares placed into a second box
Yarn needles
Rug yarn cut into 18-inch lengths

Procedure:

1. On the chalkboard or at a learning center, have the following addition sentences written out:

   $$2 + 3 = 5 \quad 5 + 5 = 10$$
   $$3 + 4 = 7 \quad 4 + 2 = 6$$
   $$9 + 1 = 10 \quad 5 + 3 = 8$$

2. Ask the children to make a necklace that represents one of the addition sentences by taking the correct number of straws and construction paper pieces from the boxes to add up the total number of pieces in the addition sentence. For example, for the combination 2 + 3 = 5, the children would take two pieces of straw cut 1½ or 2 inches long and three 1-inch construction paper squares.

3. Have the children thread a necklace onto a piece of yarn by altering a square with a straw. How many are in the new set that is a necklace?

4. Tie the yarn together and let the children wear them home.

5. Ask the children to find two new sets of materials to string a new necklace. Provide macaroni, construction paper squares, circles, beads, etc., for this new necklace.

6. Ask the children to write the sum of the pieces they used to make the necklace somewhere on the necklace.

CRAYON DRAWINGS

Materials: Newsprint, 9-by-18 inches
Crayons
Glue

Procedure:

1. Give each child one sheet of newsprint. Assign a number (1, 2, 3, 4) to each child. Have the child fold the newsprint in half.

2. On one side of the folded sheet, have the child print either 1, 2, 3, or 4 large enough to cover the paper.

3. On the second side of the folded sheet, ask the children to draw the number of objects their numbers represent. If a child has the number 2, he or she must draw two objects on his paper. The objects can be made from scrap construction paper and glued onto the folded newsprint.

4. Next, hold up a number, e.g., 6. Ask each child to find a partner who has a number that will add up to 6 if the child joins his number with his partner's.

   3 must join with a 3
   2 must join with a 4
   1 must join with a 2 and a 3

5. You may change the number you are holding to 1, 2, 3, or 5. What types of combinations can the children pair up? Possible combinations:

   1 + 1 + 1 + 1 + 1 + 1
   1 + 2 + 3
   2 + 2 + 2
   3 + 3
   4 + 1 + 1
   4 + 2
   2 + 1 + 1 + 2

RICE PAINTING

Materials: Cornmeal, rice, or white sand
Instant coffee or tea
Vegetable coloring
Heavy paper (tagboard or chipboard)
Crayons
White glue

Procedure:

1. The night before using the cornmeal, rice, or white sand, place one cup of each ingredient into plastic or tin containers. Sprinkle a few drops of vegetable coloring into the contents of the containers and stir until rice or cornmeal is colored. Make as many different colors as you wish, e.g., red, yellow, blue, green, purple. Brown will be obtained from the instant coffee or tea.

2. Instruct the children to draw, using a crayon, any number of objects on the piece of tagboard. You should specify the total number that can be drawn, for instance, 1 to 8, etc.

3. Have the children outline their design and fill in a portion of their design using white glue. Then have the children drop the colored rice or cornmeal into the area that has been covered by the glue, shaking the loose grains of rice or cornmeal back into the proper color container.

4. When the painting is completed, use the pictures as sets for making adding and subtracting sentences.

2 + 1 = 3 objects

DOUGH DOLLIES

Materials: 4 cups flour
1 cup salt
1½ to 2 cups water
Small items, such as pebbles, macaroni, etc.
Condensed milk
Food coloring

Procedure:

1. Preheat oven to 250°. Mix ingredients enough to make a soft dough. Use the macaroni, pebbles, and other items as decorations to be pressed into the Dough Dollies. Bake completed Dough Dolly for one hour. To decorate the sculpture, brush on a mixture of condensed milk with food coloring onto the Dolly.

2. Ask the children to add up the number of parts they used to create their Dough Dolly and to write an addition sentence to represent their work.

```
    2 arms
    2 legs
    1 head
    1 body
    2 eyes
  +1 mouth
    9 pieces
```

ROLLER PAINTING

Materials: Empty roll-on deodorant bottles
Tempera paint
Paper

Procedure:

1. Fill roll-on deodorant bottles with different colors of tempera paint.

2. Give the children large sheets of paper and a numeral from 1 to 9. Have the children illustrate a set that represents the numeral.

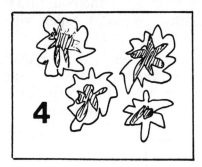   

3. Join combinations of sets to find sums of 10. Display the joined sets on a bulletin board.

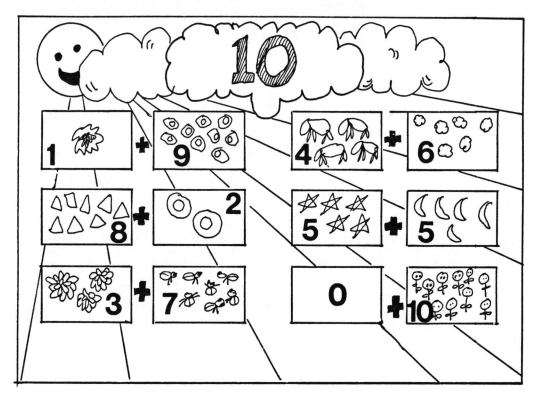

STARCH AND CHALK PAINTING

Materials: Flat pans
Liquid starch
Water
Large paintbrushes
Fingerpaint paper
Soft colored chalk

Procedure:

1. Dilute the liquid starch with small amounts of water and pour into small flat pans. Have the children rub smooth fingerpaint paper with the solution.

2. When the paper is covered with the starch solution, have them make an addition sentence with images representing the set that is being added by drawing on the paper with colored chalk. When the design dries, the starch will hold the chalk to the paper, and it will not rub off.

CONCEPT: Adding from 1 to 20 (Regrouping)

GLASS WAX WINDOWS

Materials: Glass wax
           Small sponges

Procedure:

1. Cover some school windows with glass wax. Allow to dry.
2. Instruct the children to design window patterns, using their fingers as a designing tool, which represents various addition sentences you choose to give to the class.

PEPPY THE POODLE GOES FOR A WALK

Materials: Assorted colors of construction paper
White drawing paper, 12-by-18 inches
Cotton
Scissors
Glue
Masking tape
Paper clips

Procedure:

1. Have each child make a doghouse using construction paper. Assign a number (1, 2, 3, etc.) for each child to put on his or her doghouse.

2. Instruct the children to draw and cut out a poodle. (A picture of a poodle from a magazine could be brought in for them to see.) Children can put fur (cotton) and eyes and nose (from construction paper) on their poodle. Make a collar with a tag that has their poodle's name on it.

3. Draw a line from one end of the blackboard to the other. Make a doghouse with a zero on it and the word "Peppy."

4. Tell this story:

   Peppy the Poodle lives on Poodle Paradise Lane, which you see on the blackboard. A poodle lives at every house on Poodle Paradise Lane. Peppy's address is 0 Poodle Paradise Lane.

   (You should now put Peppy's house at the beginning of the line, far left side, using masking tape.)
   Peppy is first going to visit the poodle who lives at 1 Poodle Paradise Lane.

5. The child with number 1 on his or her doghouse should put it next to Peppy's by using a paper clip to attach the dog to the house. You acknowledge the dog's name and then ask how far from home is Peppy? Continue this procedure until everyone has their doghouse on the number line. Ask the children if the numbers are getting greater or smaller.

6. Continue to make up problems to practice addition facts using the number line.

Examples: Peppy was at home and decided to go to 8 Poodle Paradise Lane. No one was home, so he went four more houses further from home. What address is he at now? Who lives there?

Peppy is hiding at the fifth house to the left of house 9. Where is he on the street?

7. Let the children take turns hiding Peppy. Have the child whisper the number of the house Peppy will be hiding in to you. Other children must guess the number by asking questions to the child. The child who hid Peppy can answer only yes or no.

Examples: Is Peppy hiding between house 0 and 15? ...Yes
Is Peppy hiding between house 0 and 10? ...No

CONCEPT: Recognizing and Completing Missing Addends

LEAFY ADDENDS—RUBBINGS

Materials: Newsprint
Scissors
Glue
Leaves
Crayons

Procedure:

1. Go outside and collect some small leaves. Try to find as many different shapes as you can.
2. Ask your teacher for some addition problems with missing addends.
3. On a sheet of newsprint, write the problem on the bottom of the page.

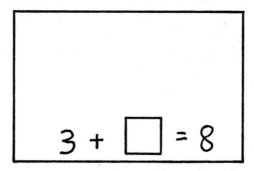

4. Make a rubbing of a pretty leaf by placing it under the newsprint and gently coloring over the leaf with crayons.

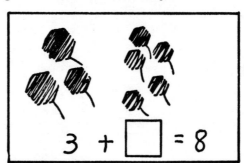

5. Finish making rubbings to show one addend in the problem, then figure out how many more times you must color the leaf to complete the problem to find the sum.

CONCEPT: Adding and Subtracting from 1 to 20

WOODBLOCK SCULPTURE

Materials: Blocks of discarded wood from a lumber yard
Paintbrushes
Tempera paint

Procedure:

1. Collect discarded pieces of wood from a lumber yard.

2. Have the children decorate the blocks by painting designs on the wood with tempera paint.

3. When the pieces have dried, use them as building blocks for movable sculpture. For example: If ten pieces belong to the total set, what happens when the teacher removes four pieces from the set? How many are left? What has happened to the sculpture?

4. If pieces of wood are not available, other objects can be used to create the sculptures, such as cereal boxes, macaroni, shells, and beads.

JUNK SCULPTURE

Materials: Swizzle sticks
Construction paper
Scissors
Plasticine clay
Beads or old, small Christmas ornaments

Procedure:

1. Using swizzle sticks and small plasticine clay balls, instruct the child to make a sculpture that uses the following combinations:

$$4 \text{ clay balls} + 15 \text{ sticks} = 19 \text{ pieces}$$
$$3 \text{ clay balls} + 4 \text{ sticks} = 7 \text{ pieces}$$

2. Have the child write the sentence that his or her sculpture represents and place it under the work when it is displayed. These sculptures may be decorated with construction paper cutouts or any dangling object the child wishes to hang onto it.

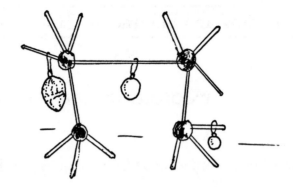

$$4 + 15 = 19$$
$$4 + 15 + (3 \text{ decorations}) = 21$$

COTTONBALL ANIMALS

Materials: Cotton balls
White glue or paste
Crayons
Construction paper

Procedure:

1. Instruct the children to take up to twenty cotton balls. Have the children divide the cotton balls into any combination on three sheets of paper.

2. Have the children glue the cotton balls onto the three separate sheets of paper. After the balls have dried, instruct the children to use the balls as animal bodies and to draw the head, legs, arms, and tails onto the body. Then, they are to write the numeral that represents the number of animals they have on their three sheets of paper.

3 +    4 +    5    = ☐

3. Ask the children to write an addition sentence that identifies their picture sentence.

4. What happens when one picture is removed? How many animals are left?

CEREAL BOX SCULPTURES

Materials: Cereal boxes, large and small
White glue

Procedure:

1. Collect empty breakfast cereal boxes. Make a sculpture by gluing the boxes together in any way the child wishes. If Child A brings in three boxes, have him make a three-box sculpture by gluing them together. If Child B brings in five boxes, have her glue them together in any way she pleases.

2. If Child A glues his boxes with Child B, they have a "new" sculpture entitled No. 8.

3. Have Children A and B glue their No. 8 sculpture to Children's C and D, whose sculpture might be named No. 10. What is the title of this new sculpture? No. 18.

4. You can direct the children by making addition sentences that describe the new sculptures.

5. An alternate plan is to have two children begin the sculpture with their sets, add two other set combinations to the basic sculpture, and eventually end up with one very large class or group sculpture. Keep track of the addends by representing the new combinations on the chalkboard. In a class of 25 students, the group sculpture might be entitled:

$$
\begin{aligned}
2 + 3 &= 5 \\
5 + 10 &= 15 \\
15 + 20 &= 35 \\
35 + 0 &= 35
\end{aligned}
$$

6. Have a group exhibition of your math/art sculptures for your school.

CONCEPT: Understanding Basic Multiplication and Division Operations

MULTIPLICATION HANDBOOKS

Materials: Any of the creative activities suggested on pages from the Handbook. (See Appendix for directions for making Multiplication/Division Handbooks.)

The children will be able to do one-, two-, and three-digit multiplication problems. You adjust the activity to the level at which the children are presently working. Choose one or many of the activities in the balance of this chapter for the children to do in order to make a Multiplication Book. A book may have various creative activities in it that are suggested in the following pages. When all of the individual pages of the book are completed, staple the entire book together or use the Japanese binding procedures to collate the book. (See the Appendix for instructions.)

Help the children to decide on the type of multiplication book they will produce. If a child is weak in multiplying different factors such as 3 × 4 = 12, have the child work on a book that focuses on the project and let the child find as many factors as possible that produce the product.

If the child is weak in using a specific multiplier such as 9, have the child work on a book that shows all the arrays with products that use 9 as the multiplier.

If the child is able to work with larger numbers using a multiplicand and multiplier, encourage the child to design a book that might show this ability.

It is important to help the children sequence their activities from simple to more difficult. Make sure the children label each page with a multiplication sentence that describes their creative work.

DIVISION HANDBOOKS

Materials: Any of the creative activities suggested on pages of the Handbook. (See Appendix for directions for making Multiplication/Division Handbooks.)

Any of the remaining activities in this section may be used for reinforcing division problems. Instruct the children to reverse the problems used for multiplication. Instead of writing a multiplication sentence at the bottom of the page, tell the children to write a division problem.

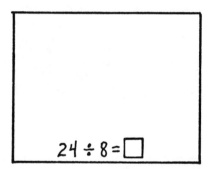

Instruct the children to make a total amount of images that represent the dividend. Then instruct the children to use the divisor as a rule for segregating the total number of images. This will produce the quotient.

Procedure:

1. Cut out from construction paper twenty-four fish or twenty-four faces or twenty-four bugs.

2. Sort the fish, faces, or bugs into eight piles. The number "8" tells you how many piles you should put the twenty-four images into.

3. NOTE: If the teacher gives the child a problem with a remainder, please instruct the child that each pile must have the same amount of images in it. If there are not enough images to sort into piles, then what is remaining must be indicated on the design as the remainder.

CONCEPT: Multiplying and Dividing Through 9 × 9

CONSTRUCTION PAPER PATTERNS

Materials: Construction paper
Scissors
Glue

Procedure:

1. Decide on the multiplication problem you will work on in this activity.
2. Write the problem at the bottom of the paper.
3. Cut out images such as fish, flowers, bugs, or butterflies that will represent your multiplication sentence.
4. Paste or glue the images onto the construction paper. Save each page you make for your book.

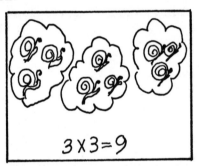

SEALED NATURE PATTERNS

Materials: Interesting forms of flat leaves, flower petals, weeds, and grasses
Wax paper
Iron (Caution to Teacher: Do not allow students to use the iron themselves as burns may result.)
Crayon
Newsprint

Procedure:

1. Tell the children to cut two sheets of wax paper that are of equal size and the same size as the multiplication book.

2. The children then lay one sheet of wax paper on the newspaper and arrange the plant life on the wax paper to represent the multiplication sentence.

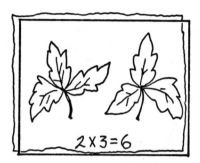

3. Next, the children place the other waxed sheet over the first, covering the plant life pattern.

4. The children place newspaper on top of the wax paper. Then the teacher irons over the second sheet with a warm flat iron. This will seal the waxed sheets together, preserving the plant life.

5. The children write the multiplication sentence with crayon on the bottom of the page that describes the design they made.

CRAYON ETCHING

Materials: Construction paper (light color)
Scraping tool (such as a stick, nail, or scissors)
Crayons
Tissue or cloth

Procedure:

1. The children cover the entire top of the paper with a heavy coat of brightly colored crayon in either a free or planned design. The heavier the colors are applied, the better the result. No definite drawing or design is necessary at this point.

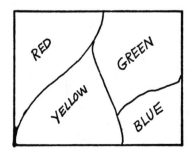

2. They crayon over the brightly colored surface with black, violet, or any dark color until no original color shows. By first rubbing the crayon-covered surface with a piece of Kleenex tissue or cloth, the dark crayons stick better.

3. The children decide on their multiplication sentence and represent it by scratching or scraping through the dark surface to the colors beneath. A child may decide to scratch a school of fish to represent his or her sentence. Tell the children to be sure to scratch in their multiplication sentence at the bottom of the picture.

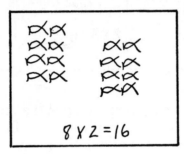

SOAP ERASER PRINTS

Materials: Pencil with a sharp point
Soap gum eraser
Printing pad
Newsprint

Procedure:

1. Each child decides on a multiplication problem to be worked out.

2. The child scratches out a design on one surface of the soap gum eraser with a sharp pencil point.

3. Other designs are scratched out on the remaining surfaces.

4. The stamp pad is used to print a design on a sheet of newsprint.

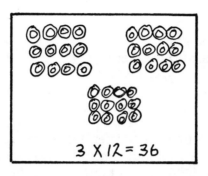

CRAYON ON CLOTH—
MAKING A HEAD SCARF OR PLACE MAT

Materials: Crayons
Piece of muslin
Iron (for teacher only)

Procedure:

1. The children choose a multiplication sentence to represent.

2. They draw a design showing that multiplication problem on the muslin in order to make a pattern. The drawing is done directly on the cloth using considerable pressure with the crayon.

3. Melt the crayon into the cloth for each child by placing it between two sheets of newspaper and ironing it with a warm iron. The color then becomes semi-permanent and can be washed in cold water.

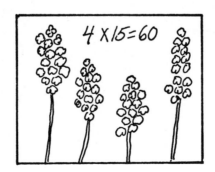

PAPER FINGER PUPPETS

Materials: Construction paper
Paste or white glue
Crayons or felt-tip markers
Tape
Scissors

Procedure:

1. Tell the children to find a friend and make up a short play to be presented to the class about multiplication facts. They can make some finger puppets to be used as characters in the play.

2. To make the finger puppet, tell the children to roll a strip of paper to form a tube that will fit their fingers snugly.

3. The tube is then taped and pasted together.

4. Features such as faces and hats can be added with other pieces of paper and with crayons. Students can cut into the paper tube by folding the paper and cutting it with a scissor. They can also make puppets from paper cups.

5. A variation would be to use old gloves and cut the fingers from the gloves, decorating by gluing features onto the gloved finger.

Section 5
PLACE VALUE

To the teacher

The activities in this section center on children's ability to demonstrate through visual images their ability to perform place value interpretations. Stories are used to reinforce place value notions and children are encouraged to design, write, and bind their own place value books.

The combination of a fantasy situation and the abstraction of mathematics provides the children with a unique mathematical experience. Some children may find it difficult to translate numbers into concrete images. This can be easily remedied by explaining to them that the symbol used to represent the property of numbers is a traditional symbol. Although several activities emphasize place value, they also employ computation.

Encouraging children to design and create their own symbols representing the number is a refreshing way to look at the arithmetic they are learning. The story of the Frodes and Squirmin' Sherman can be elaborated upon at your discretion. The Frodes represent the ones place and Squirmin' Sherman represents the tens place. You may want to use plastic balls to represent Frodes and a sock puppet that holds exactly ten balls to represent Squirmin' Sherman.

Encourage the children to make Frode and Squirmin' Sherman books and perhaps their very own puppets. Later, translate the Frodes and Squirmin' Sherman story into the Bug Army Story. The variation is motivating, but the method is reinforcing.

The section also provides you with worksheet ideas that can be easily reproduced. These worksheets are designed to provide children with practice in basic computation. The exercises use a creative symbol for each place value concept while applying addition and subtraction operations.

Visual imagery is a form of symbolic communication. Having the children draw the objects will inform you of the children's progress and ability to grasp the concept. Drawing out the addition sentences or the multiplication arrays helps children to understand place value and basic operations.

Be creative with these activities. A common question regarding the Frodes and Squirmin' Sherman story is where does the Squirmin' Sherman go when he is empty? Well, be inventive. Try responding by saying he goes where all Squirmin' Shermans go—he just disappears into the grass.

CONCEPT: Designating Place Value in 1's, 10's, and 100's

FRODES AND SQUIRMIN' SHERMAN
(AN ADVENTURE IN PLACE VALUE)

Materials: 2-inch circles or squares cut from construction paper
Crayons
Magic markers
Yarn
Beans
Buttons

Procedure:

1. Read the following story:

The Frodes and Squirmin' Sherman

Once upon a time, there was a colony of Frodes that lived near a huge rock. This is what one Frode looks like:

The Frodes loved to sun themselves. Every day some Frodes would go out on the rock and sun themselves. However, they were very careful not to sun on the rock where there were too many Frodes out for the day. They knew it was safe for nine Frodes to sit upon the rock at one time. Yet, some days more than nine Frodes would crawl upon the rock to sun themselves. The reason they were careful not to have too many Frodes on the rock was because of Squirmin' Sherman. Squirmin' Sherman was a creature that loved to eat Frodes. So, he would watch the rock and count each Frode as it came out to sun. He could eat only ten Frodes at one time. He never could eat eleven or eight or three Frodes. He always ate Frodes ten at a time. This is what Squirmin' Sherman looks like:

However, Squirmin' Sherman had to watch out for Grizzly Grenelda. What do you suppose she does? That's right, she likes to decorate herself with ten Squirmin' Shermans. Not eight or eleven or four, but ten at a time.

Frodes are the ones place. Squirmin' Shermans are the tens place. Grizzly Greneldas are the hundreds place.

The total number of Frodes is _____.

2. Have the children decorate a Frode (2-inch circle or square).

3. Design a bulletin board that displays a large Squirmin' Sherman and Frode sitting on a rock.

4. Have the children pin their Frodes to the Frodes' rock. Count the Frodes that are sunning on the rock. Place the numeral representing the number of Frodes on the rock.

5. When ten Frodes are sunning on the rock, Squirmin' Sherman eats them. Place the ten 2-inch circles into the Squirmin' Sherman on the bulletin board. Be sure Squirmin' Sherman is large enough to hold ten Frodes.

6. Design and introduce Frode and Squirmin' Sherman worksheets. Try making a Frode and Squirmin' Sherman puppet. Invent a way of teaching subtraction by regrouping using a Squirmin' Sherman and Frode story.

Example of Bulletin Board

THREE BLIND MICE

Materials: One large sheet of paper per child
Crayons or construction paper
Envelopes or milk cartons
Toothpicks
Rubberbands
Glue

Procedure:

1. Three blind mice are collecting toothpicks to build a house. The mice can't see, but they know when something is heavy. The littlest mouse can carry only nine toothpicks. When he gets ten, he puts them together in a bunch and gives them to the next mouse who is bigger than he is. The middle mouse can hold nine bunches of ten. If he gets ten bunches, he puts them together in a big bunch and gives them to the biggest mouse. The biggest mouse can hold nine big bunches.

2. Have the children make each mouse from largest to smallest on the large sheet of paper. An envelope or milk carton should be glued below each mouse.

3. Give each child a bunch of toothpicks. Can the little mouse hold all of them? How many should he give to the middle mouse and how many should the little mouse keep? Instruct the children to count ten toothpicks, put a rubberband around them, and insert them into the proper mouse pocket.

4. The children can practice with different numbers and then move on to the hundreds place. Index cards with numbers could be placed on paper also to correspond with the toothpicks and groups of toothpicks.

THE PLACE VALUE BUG ARMY BOOK

Materials: Construction paper
Scissors
Crayons
Glue
Seeds

Procedure:

1. Make a book from construction paper that will show and tell the proper name of a number. All of the numbers that are in the ones place are called bug soldiers. Only nine bug soldiers may be in the ones place. Make some soldiers about 2 inches high from construction paper. Give them soldier hats. Cut them out and paste them on a page of a Place Value Bug Army Book. Have the children write the number of soldiers you made on each page.

2. Make some bug sergeants. Sergeants stand in the tens place. No soldier can stand in the sergeant's place. Make some sergeants from construction paper and crayons and give them a sergeant's hat. Cut them out and paste them on a page of the Place Value Bug Army Book. Instruct the children to write the number of sergeants they made in the tens place and the number of soldiers that will accompany the sergeants. Remember, only one to nine soldiers can stand in the soldier's place; ten soldiers will not fit. If the children have ten soldiers, instruct them to automatically change them into one sergeant.

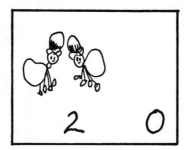

3. Make some pages for the book that show the following numbers by using the bug sergeants and soldiers:

42, 31, 19

4. After some pages show the tens and one places, have the children make some bug generals to show the hundreds place. They can design a very fancy hat for the generals and decorate it with seeds. Show the following numbers by using generals, sergeants, and soldiers:

432, 625, 511

For fun, read *Drummer Hoff* by B. Emberly (Englewood Cliffs, N.J.: Prentice-Hall, Inc., 1967) to the children.

CONCEPT: Adding Three-Digit Numbers—Regrouping

THE PLACE VALUE BUG ARMY MARCHES ON

Materials: Construction paper
Scissors
Crayons
Seeds
Glue or paste

Procedure:

1. The Place Value Bug Army is growing. Show the following addition problem by making soldiers, sergeants, and generals. Add the pages to the Place Value Bug Army Book.

$$\begin{array}{r} 485 \\ +315 \\ \hline 800 \end{array}$$

2. Provide addition problems appropriate for the children's level.

CONCEPT: Subtracting Three-Digit Numbers—Regrouping

THE PLACE VALUE BUG ARMY GOES TO A PICNIC

Materials: Construction paper
Glue or paste
Scissors
Crayons
Seeds

Procedure:

1. The Place Value Bug Army goes to a picnic. They meet the Frodes. Have the children add some pages to the Place Value Bug Army Book by showing the answers to the following problems.

2. The Place Value Bug Army had 321 soldiers go to the picnic. The Frodes bug chased away 109 of the Place Value Bugs to keep them off their picnic lunch. How many bugs were left?

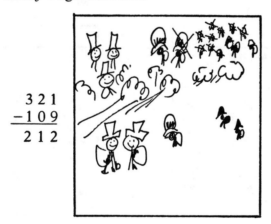

$$\begin{array}{r} 3\ 2\ 1 \\ -\ 1\ 0\ 9 \\ \hline 2\ 1\ 2 \end{array}$$

3. Provide some subtraction problems that can add to the book or have the children make up their own.

4. Encourage the children to finish the story.

CONCEPT: Adding and Subtracting Three-Digit Numbers— Without Regrouping

CREATIVE THREE-DIGIT PROBLEMS

Materials: Reproducible worksheets

Procedure:

1. Make enlargements of the worksheets provided here and have the children work them out.

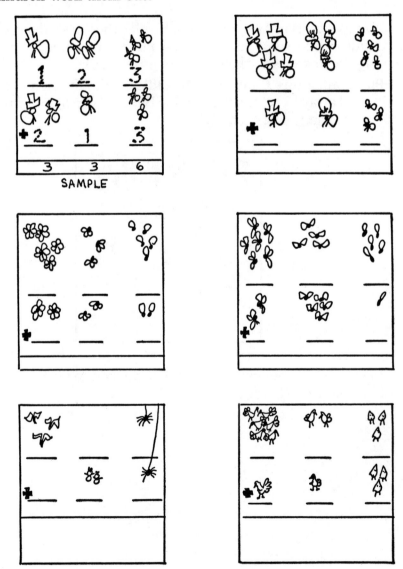

SAMPLE

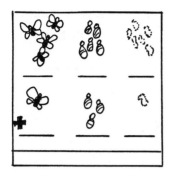

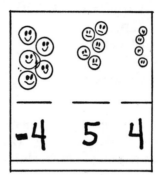

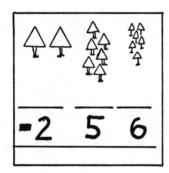

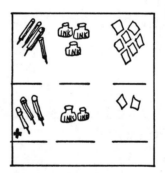

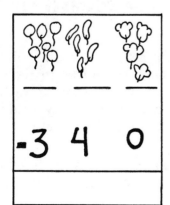

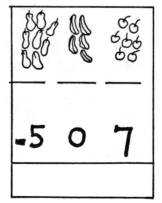

CONCEPT: Computing Four-Place Addition Problems—
              Regrouping

ALL-STAR QUIZ SHOW

Materials: Poster paper
               Large piece of cloth (to decorate table)
               Tape
               Streamers
               Table
               Chairs

Procedure:

1. As a group project, decorate a long table where contestants in a quiz show will sit behind. Also as a group, decorate the background. (Example: Name of show, slogans, colorful decorations.)

2. Choose five children to be on the panel at a time. Give the children an advance warning by informing them that they will be in the contest. (Everyone will get a chance; however, not on the same day.) Instruct those who will be contestants to choose an occupation they would like to role-play. Children then dress to fit that role (i.e., doctor, engineer, farmer, clown).

3. Day of Contest! As the contestants are changing into their costumes, give the remaining children a sheet of paper containing all four-place

addition problems. These are the problems the contestants will be asked to solve. Let the audience (rest of class) compute the problems. Place a sheet of paper and a pencil at each contestant's seat.

4. Bring in the contestants. You will be the moderator the first time the quiz show is conducted. After the first time, you may want to choose a child to act as moderator.

5. As on television, introduce the name of the show. Introduce the contestants and have them tell something about themselves describing their line of work.

6. Announce the first four-place addition problem (with regrouping). The first contestant to complete the problem raises his or her hand. Let other contestants finish before calling on the first one who finished.

7. The first child to finish announces his or her answer. Children at their seats should applaud if they think it is a correct answer. A correct answer is worth 10 points. If the answer is not correct, all other children must show their answers. All contestants have a chance to receive 10 points if their answer is correct.

8. The first child to receive 50 points wins. An inexpensive prize or a privilege could be given to the winner. This activity can be adapted to multiplication and division problems.

9. Adapt this contestant activity to "Hollywood Squares." You moderate by presenting a difficult four-digit problem with answer. The contestant asks someone in the Hollywood Squares box if the answer is correct or not.

CONCEPT: Computing Four-Place Subtraction Problems—
Without Regrouping

THE DISAPPEARING MICE BOOK

Materials: White paper, 12-by-24 inches
Colored construction paper
Ink pads
Hole punch
Yarn

Procedure:

1. Have children make subtraction books by folding six white sheets of paper in half. Also, fold colored paper in half for the book cover.

2. Place white sheets inside the cover and punch holes approximately **1** inch apart from top to bottom of folder side. Bind your book with yarn by sewing in and out of the holes using the Japanese binding procedure described in the Appendix.

3. Leave the first page blank. This page will be the title page for the title of the book and the author's name. The title could be decided after the children have finished their books.

4. On the top of the next page (do not use the back of pages) have the children write a four-place subtraction problem that does not involve regrouping. Instruct the children to allow enough space between each number in order to provide space for four columns extending from each side of the page. Have the children label each column indicating place value.

4	6	8	9
−1	4	3	5
Thousands	Hundreds	Tens	Ones

5. Using an ink pad, have the children make thumbprint mice that represent mice in each "cage" (the number before any are subtracted). Instruct the children to use their little fingers for each mouse.

THOUSANDS	HUNDREDS	TENS	ONES

6. Instruct the children to subtract by crossing out the number of mice the problem is dictating. Make sure the children work from right to left.

7. All following pages should contain subtraction problems where regrouping is necessary.

CONCEPT: Relating Monetary System with Base-10 Place
Value System

THE MONEY MUNCHING ROBOT

Materials: One large box
Lots of decoration

Procedure:

1. Design and decorate a large money changing robot box. Example:

2. One child sits inside the box and operates the "mechanism" of the robot.

3. Have each child create a money datum list on a sheet of paper.
"I have 11 dimes, 5 nickels, and 14 pennies. How much do I have?"

4. Have the child insert the money datum list into the "in" opening. The child inside must figure out in dollars and cents how much money was inserted.

5. He or she sends the total amount through the "out" opening, with best wishes for the day.

6. This activity will give the child sitting in the box practice in changing money into dollars and cents.

MONEY CHANGING GAME

Materials: Typing paper
Sharp pencil point
Scissors
Stamps for: 1 penny, 1 nickel, 1 dime, 1 quarter, 1 half-dollar, 1 silver dollar. (If coin stamps are unavailable, use "play" coins or cardboard cutouts.)
Envelopes

Procedure:

1. Have each child make three or four of each of the coins mentioned above by using a rubber coin stamp of the front and back of the coin, cutting out the coins and gluing the front and back together.

2. Collect all coins.

3. Put different amounts of coins in envelopes and then assign one envelope per child.

4. Instruct the children to "find a partner" and determine the amount of money they have (don't mix the coins together, though). The partners with the most money receive a point.

5. Instruct the children to find another partner and proceed in the same manner as before.

6. Form groups of three and determine which group has the most money (each member of the winning group receives one point). Repeat this procedure by forming groups of four.

7. Determine who received the most points, the most amount of money, and the "most wealthy" groups.

Section 6
SIMPLE FRACTIONS

To the teacher

Fractions may be introduced in the primary mathematics curriculum. Usually lessons begin with simple fractions such as halves, thirds, and fourths and are aimed at helping children understand that fractions are parts of a whole. This concept may take on different meanings.

One meaning of a fraction symbol is that it signifies a representation of part of a collection or set of objects. "Felt Wall Hanging," "Stitchery Fractions," and "Fraction Collage" activities are excellent for reinforcing this meaning.

Fractions also represent the quotient of two whole numbers. "Loop De Doos" and "Making a Pizza," along with other activities in the chapter, reinforce this meaning.

The activity encouraging children to make fraction books may motivate children to take a serious look at fraction problems and symbolism. The activities allow the children to explore many forms of media used in visual expression and change the standard paper-and-pencil tasks to crayons, paint, and muslin. This change in itself stimulates the children's curiosity about the fraction lesson.

CONCEPT: Understanding and Recognizing the Simple Fractions ¼, ½, ⅓

FAMILY FRACTIONS

Materials: Ten shoe boxes
Wooden tongue depressors
Glue
Construction paper (multicolored) and/or white paper

Procedure:

1. Label the end of shoe boxes whole, halves, thirds, fourths, fifths, sixths, sevenths, eighths, ninths, and tenths.

2. Have children decorate the shoe boxes as homes. Each house is for a family. The family's name is on the end of the box.

3. Instruct the children to make the people that live in the house by making stick puppets from construction paper or white drawing paper and gluing the figures onto wooden tongue depressors.

4. How many persons live in the Eighths house? How many live in the Sixths house?

5. Encourage the children to make up puppet plays that show how many ½ of the "Eights" family might be. What would ⅓ of the "Sixths" family consist of? Who lives in the "Ones" family?

FRACTION BOOKS

Instructions to the Teacher:

The children will be able to identify simple fractions and will be able to add and subtract these fractions.

The following activities may be adjusted to the level at which the children are presently working. Choose one or many of the following art activities for the children to participate in so they can make a Fraction Book. Each book may have a variety of art activities or it may be a repetition of a few art activities. When the children feel the book is completed and you feel the individual child has worked out areas of problem solving in which the child is weak, staple the entire book together.

Help the children to decide on the type of Fraction Book they will produce. If the child is weak in identifying simple fractions such as ½, ¼, or ¾, have the child work on activities that center around this objective. Encourage the children to reproduce as many visual representations of simple fractions as is possible. An individual child's book may be titled *My Book of Simple Fractions* or as shown:

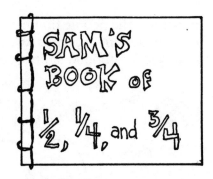

If a child is weak in equivalent fractions, focus all of the activities on solving this problem. The child's book title will then become *My Book of Equivalents of ½.*

It is important to help children sequence their creative activities from simple to more difficult representations of fractions. Make sure each page is labeled with the fraction sentence that describes the fraction problem with which the individual child is involved.

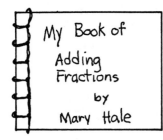  

Feel free to examine some of the activities in the multiplication section of this book. Many of these activities may be used to reinforce work with fractions by changing the objective of the problem and adjusting the activity to meet the children's needs.

Bind the fraction books by using the Japanese Binding Method described in the Appendix.

PAPER SCRIPT DESIGNS

Materials: Scissors
Crayons
Newsprint
Construction paper

Procedure:

1. Fold some newsprint in half.

2. Have the children write a word or their name in script with a crayon along the creased edge. The crayon will ensure enough thickness of line to permit the cutting of the letters on both sides.

3. Cut on both sides of the crayoned line, making sure each letter is held together by the fold.

4. Paste the letters that have been cut out on contrasting colored paper. (Note: A word containing a letter that extends below the line, such as f, g, j, p, q, or y, must be written above the fold so only the extension of that letter reaches the fold.)

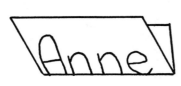 

5. Paste one-half of the back side on a sheet of construction paper and print a problem on the bottom. You might have the students write ½ + ½ = 1 or ½ + ¼ = ¾. Display the finished papers on a bulletin board.

MOSAIC PICTURES

Materials: Scissors
White glue
Construction paper
Pencil

Procedure:

1. Decide on the fraction problem the children will work out to make a mosaic picture.
2. Divide the construction paper with a pencil into areas that will represent the portions of the fraction.

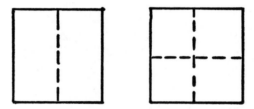

3. Study the areas and decide what design will go into each section. Cut out small pieces of colored construction paper and paste them into a design for each of the areas.
4. Write the fraction sentence that described the work.

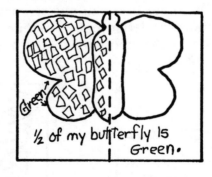

CUT PAPER DESIGNS

Materials: Newsprint or tissue paper
Construction paper
Scissors
Glue

Procedure:

1. Decide on a simple fraction for the children to work on. Have them fold the paper into sections that represent that fraction.

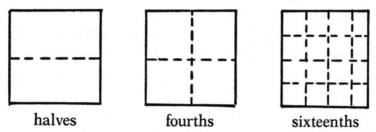

halves   fourths   sixteenths

2. The children then cut numerous small shapes out of the paper until there is more paper cut away than there is remaining. They do not cut through the entire paper.

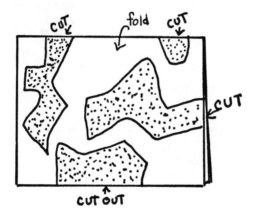

3. Tell the children to unfold the paper carefully so as not to tear it when opening.
4. The design is glued carefully by putting dabs of glue to points of the design and gluing it to a contrasting piece of construction paper.
5. The children can make as many different designs as they wish for their Fraction Book. Tell them to write the fraction that describes their designs.

WAX PAPER DESIGNS

Materials: Wax paper
Staples
Scissors
White glue
Paper clip
Construction paper

Procedure:

1. Decide on the fraction the children will represent.

2. Cut a sheet of wax paper to fit over a piece of construction paper.

3. Fold the wax paper into thirds, fourths, eighths, or sixteenths.

4. Staple or glue the piece of wax paper to a dark piece of construction paper. Try to leave a border by cutting away about an inch of wax paper.

5. Use an opened paper clip to scratch a design carefully into each section of the folded wax paper. Be careful not to cut through the wax paper. The color from the construction paper will appear when you have scratched the surface of the wax paper.

⅙ of my design has a dog in it.
⁴⁄₆ or ⅔ of my design has pigs in it.
⅙ of my design has a bug in it.

SPLITTING AREAS

Materials: Contrasting pieces of construction paper, such as black and white, red and green, or yellow and blue

Procedure:

1. Use a dark color of construction paper. Cut a shape from it.

2. Cut the shape into pieces to represent a fraction and paste it onto the contrasting color.

3. Write a description of the fraction pieces on the bottom of the page.

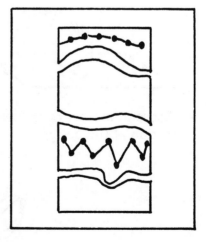

This is made up of 4 pieces.
1 piece is ¼ of the design.
2 pieces are 2/4 or ½ of the design.
3 pieces are ¾ of the design.
4 pieces are 4/4 or the entire design.

4. Make other shapes and ask the children to write a description of the fractions using more pieces. For example, can they write a description of a design cut into 8 pieces? 12 pieces? 32 pieces?

LOOP DE DOOS

Materials: Colored construction paper
Scissors
Clear tape

Procedure:

1. Decide on the fraction the children want to represent.

2. Cut the colored construction paper into ¼-inch or ½-inch strips. Cut out exactly the right number of strips that will represent the fraction. For example: If the fraction is ³⁄₆, then the children will need 6 strips; 3 will be one color and 3 will be a second color.

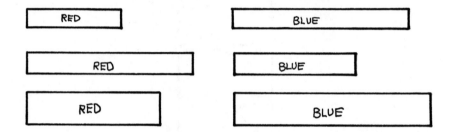

3. Form the strips into numerous shapes, fastening the ends together with paste or clear tape.

4. Choose a number of shapes that are one *color* to represent ½ or ¼ or a fraction of the design.

5. Glue them onto a contrasting sheet of construction paper and make the design.

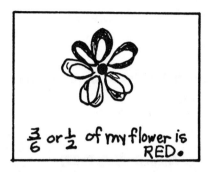

6. Write the fraction sentence underneath the design.

7. Tell the children to make up other Loop De Doo designs to represent other fractions.

PAPER WEAVING

Materials: Colored construction paper
Scissors
Paste

Procedure:

1. Decide on the fraction the children will represent.

2. Cut a series of slits into a large sheet of colored construction paper. Make sure they *do not* cut completely through the paper.

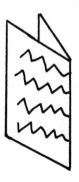 

3. Tell the children to cut strips of colored paper that will represent the fraction. Explain that if the fraction is ⅕, then that means they must cut five equal strips of paper. One of the strips will be one color and four of the strips will be another color.

4. The children then weave the strips of paper through the slits in the paper.

5. They hold the strips of paper in place with a spot of glue.

6. Help the children to write the fraction on the bottom of the page by stating it in a sentence.

> ⅓ of my weaving is blue or ¾ of my weaving is yellow and ¼ of the weaving is green.

MAKING A PIZZA

Materials: Unbleached muslin
Iron (teacher is to use iron)
Crayons
Newsprint

Procedure:

1. Decide on the fraction the children will use.

2. Draw a large circle with crayon on a piece of unbleached muslin.

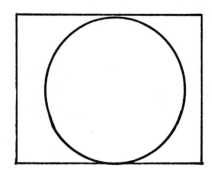

3. Divide the pizza into the proper number of sections suggested by the denominator in the fraction.

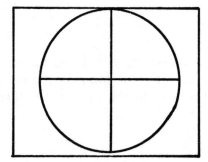

4. If the pizza is divided into fourths, then place the following ingredients into one-fourth of the pizza by having the children draw and color in the ingredients with crayon: olives, mushrooms, sausages, plain.

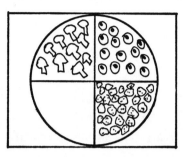

5. Have the children bring the muslin to you so you can press it between two sheets of newspaper with a warm iron. The crayon will melt into the muslin and the children will have a pizza scarf or flag. Be sure they write the fraction sentence that describes the pizza somewhere on the muslin.

INK PAD PRINTS

Materials: Newsprint
Two colors of ink pads
Printing tool

Procedure:

1. Decide on two fractions for the children to represent.
2. Press a finger, the heel or side of a hand, or any item to be printed on the paper into the ink pad. Use two different colors to represent the fraction.
3. Press the inked area to the newsprint paper. Make a design that represents the two fractions. Be sure to write the fractions at the bottom of the design. Tell the children to decide which fraction is greater and to use the appropriate symbol.
4. Sticks, jar lids, pencil erasers, or any small flat item may be used to make an interesting printing tool.

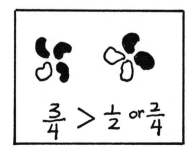

FELT WALL HANGINGS

Materials: Felt
            Burlap
            Scissors
            Glue

Procedure:

1. Decide on the fraction to represent.
2. Cut out a design from the felt pieces that represents the fraction problem.
3. The children glue the felt pieces onto the burlap for their wall hanging. Be sure they write the fraction sentence in their Fraction Book.

R = red   y = yellow

B = blue   o = orange

G = green   b = black

Fraction sentences that describe the wall hanging include:

⅓ of my flowers are red
⅔ of my flowers are blue
³⁄₃ of my stems are green
³⁄₆ of my leaves are yellow *or*
½ of my leaves are orange
¹⁄₁ of my ground is black

FRACTION COLLAGE

Materials: One large piece of paper 22-by-28 inches
               Old magazines
               Glue

Procedure:

1. Have each child make a collage that tells all about himself or herself.

2. After the collage is finished, have the children count the number of pieces they used to make the whole collage. For example:

This collage used 25 pieces.

3. On a sheet of paper have them find out what fraction of their collage is pictures of:

Attribute	Fraction
girls	14/25
dogs	2/25
snakes	0/25
red in picture	24/25
black-and-white pictures	3/25
adults	
flowers	
soft things	
squares	
houses	
babies	
Indians	
trees	
color blue	
food	
sports	
(add as many variables as the teacher wishes)	

Section 7
MEASUREMENT

To the teacher

Measurement is one of our most important mathematical tools. We use it daily without being aware of our intuitive abilities to measure objects using nonstandard and standard units. The activities is this section provide children with experiences in measuring length, perimeters, area, volume, and weight.

Some activities foster skills in following directions. Children at all ages need experiences in developing listening skills that reinforce their ability to process verbal information. These lessons on measurement improve listening skills along with the application of linear measurement skills. The suggested activities may motivate you to expand specific listening procedures into more elaborate lessons personally designed by the students using their own original sets of directions.

CONCEPT: Measuring Perimeters and Area Using Nonstandard Units

POPCORN RULERS

Materials: Popcorn
Tapestry needle
Objects
Thread

Procedure:

1. String popcorn on thread. Count the number of kernels on the thread. Each child will have a different sum.

2. Use the popcorn ruler to measure around things.
   a. your tummy
   b. your head
   c. your wrist
   d. your ankle
   e. your friend's tummy, head, wrist, ankle

3. Record the popcorn lengths.

COTTONBALL MEASURING RULER

Materials: Cotton balls
White glue

Procedure:

1. Have the children glue down cotton balls on a long strip of adding machine paper by placing them one next to the other. Make the ruler long, perhaps up to 100 in number. The white glue will hold the cotton balls securely.

2. Number each ball in sequence. The ruler will be flexible enough to bend so that perimeters can be measured and recorded.

3. Measure area by placing cotton balls in each region and counting the balls. Measure the area in cotton balls for the following:
    a. On a large sheet of paper, have a friend trace the child's body.

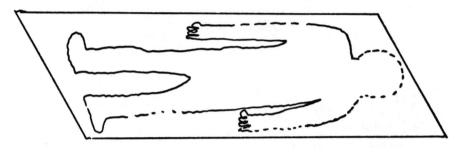

How many cotton balls will it take to cover the body?
    b. Trace a hand or foot and measure the area in cotton balls.

TICKY-TACK AND STOMP-STOMP

Materials: Crayons
Rubber cement
Scissors
Construction paper
Plastic gloves, usually used to handle food or to dye hair (cut the fingers off and give two per child)

Procedure:

Tell a story:

1. Ticky-Tack is a bird. Have the children make a bird's foot from construction paper by drawing the bird's claws, cutting them out, and rubber-cementing them onto plastic finger puppet. Make a pair. Be sure to use rubber cement; white glue will not work.

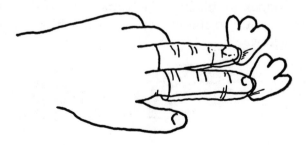

2. Stomp-Stomp is a bear. Have the children make one huge bear paw by drawing it on construction paper.

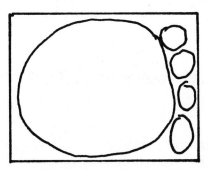

3. Have the children measure the length, perimeter, and area of the bear paw by walking the length, perimeter, and region with the two finger puppets.

4. The children may want to measure other objects using Ticky-Tack puppet feet. Have the children make up Ticky-Tack and Stomp-Stomp stories as they measure the perimeters of desks, trays, jars, tummies, and other interesting objects.

CONCEPT: Measuring and Comparing Lengths of Various Objects

AN ARBITRARY MEASURING FOOT

Materials: White construction paper
Multicolored felt-tipped pens or crayons

Procedure:

1. Have child trace his or her foot on a sheet of paper and draw a face on it.

2. Cut out the feet. Have children measure various objects using their own feet as standard lengths. Record how many foot sizes it takes to measure:
   a. their best friend
   b. a table
   c. the teacher
   d. a desk
   e. a plant

3. Have children compare lengths of the same object measured by several children. Were there any differences?

4. Give each child a paper clip. How many paper clip lengths does it take to measure their foot drawing? Record results.

5. Give them a ruler and have each of them measure their foot in inches and in meters.

KEEP A RECORD

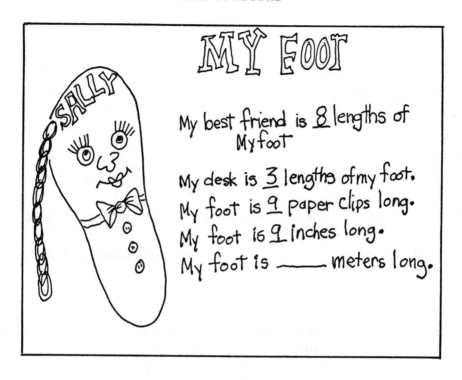

NATURE'S NICHES

Materials: Twigs, leaves, and weeds
Large sheet of white paper, 22-by-28 inches

Prodecure:

1. Randomly give each child a bunch of dried grasses, weeds, twigs, and leaves.

2. Have them order them from shortest to longest on paper. Glue them down and make a forest scene from dried pieces.

THE LONG AND SHORT OF IT ALL

Materials: Crayons
Tongue depressors
Empty cereal boxes
Shells and other objects with varying shapes and sizes

Procedure:

1. Have the children line up from shortest to tallest in a straight line as fast as they can.
2. Send the children on a scavenger hunt for the smallest object and the longest object they can hold in one hand.
3. Send the children outside and compare the lengths of the smallest shadow they can find against the longest shadow.
4. Give each child a bunch of old crayons. Compare lengths from shortest to longest.
5. Give each child about a dozen wooden tongue depressors. Working in teams of four, have the children measure various objects in the room by laying the depressors end to end. Make sure the children keep a record of their findings. The team with the longest measurement wins the game. (Most likely they will vary according to how straight the sticks were laid.)

6. Collect empty cereal boxes. Have the children order them from shortest to tallest.
7. Collect shells, objects of various interesting shapes, and order them from shortest to tallest.

Note: Each of these procedures may be used independently or combined with others for a series of games to show "the long and short of it all."

THE POTATO PRINT RULER

Materials: One potato per child
White construction paper
Tempera
A carving tool
Paintbrush
Tray for paint

Procedure:

1. Cut each potato in half for the children.

2. Instruct the children to carve a pattern into the potato.

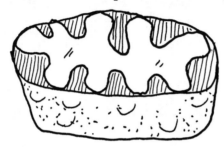

3. Cover the surface of the potato with a thin layer of tempera paint.

4. Press potato on a sheet of paper to produce the print. Once the child acquires the skill of producing a print, instruct him or her to make a potato print ruler by printing the pattern carefully along a straight line and repeating the potato print end to end.

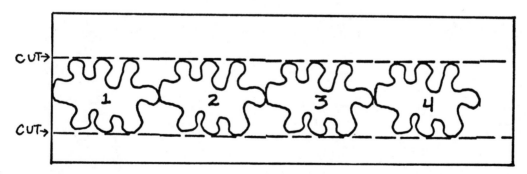

5. Cut out ruler.

6. Instruct the children to measure and compare lengths of various objects and people in the classroom. Record lengths.

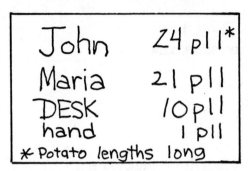

7. Use the potato print ruler to measure the perimeter of objects, too.

CONCEPT: Balancing and Ordering by Weight

HEAVY PEOPLE

Materials: Rocks, pebbles (light colored and smooth)
Tempera paint or magic markers
Acrylic spray

Procedure:

1. Have each child collect various rocks and pebbles (no more than ten).

2. Have each child put the rocks in order from lightest to heaviest according to weight by placing one rock in each hand and judging which is heavier.

3. Have the children paint or draw a face on each rock; then spray with acrylic spray.

4. Have the class order the rocks and pebbles as a group from lightest to heaviest. Assign a number to each rock in proper sequence.

1   **2**   **3**   **4**   **5**   **6**

IDEAS FOR WEIGHING IN

1. Look in the cupboard. Record weights on cans and order from heaviest to lightest.
2. Gather natural objects. Weigh on small scale and record weights from lightest to heaviest on a weight line.

feather	½ oz.
twig	3 oz.
stone	7 oz.
shoe	2 lbs.

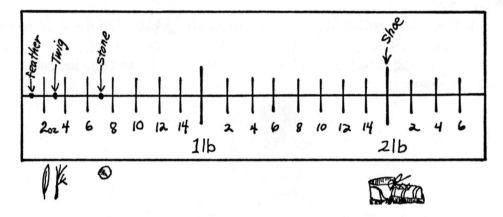

GEOMETRY

To the teacher

Geometric figures and shapes are found all around in the physical world. Children are constantly referring to various shapes, noting the inside and outside of objects, and identifying patterns. These terms illustrate the readiness skills, which prepare the children for their first introduction into the mathematical world of Geometry.

Geometry in the early grades helps children better understand their world. Early exposure to geometric models helps them understand many arithmetic concepts and principles, especially in the area of measurement.

The following activities are designed to reinforce figure recognition and construction and to introduce some study of topology. The Closed and Open Shape Tree activity aids children in distinguishing between closed and open curves, while helping them classify basic shapes. After such an activity you may want to develop the lesson into an introduction to various three-dimensional polygons. Poly-polygons provides patterns that are classroom reproducible. Children can construct these figures themselves. The section ends with two activities for the more advanced child who demonstrates an interest in surfaces and figures. The two topology activities, Flexigons and Mobius Strips, may appeal to the teacher wishing to expand his or her knowledge in the field. The exceptionally bright child will find these activities fascinating.

CONCEPT: Reproducing Common Shapes by Pencil Drawings

PAPER RUBBINGS AND STORY STARTERS

Materials: Construction paper
           Scissors
           White typing paper
           Rubber cement

Procedure:

1. Draw some basic shapes such as a circle, square, triangle, and rectangle on construction paper. Cut out the shapes. Arrange them on a sheet of white construction paper. Instruct the children to make an object only using the basic Euclidean shapes.

2. Place a sheet of white typing paper over the construction paper design and rub gently with a crayon to produce an image.

3. Have the children write a five-page story about their designs using this method to illustrate the story. Bind into a book.

STRAW BLOWING ARTY SHAPES

Materials: White drawing paper
One straw cut 4 inches long
Box of watercolors
String

Procedure:

1. On a sheet of white drawing paper (9-by-12 inches) have the children draw on each sheet: a large circle, a square, a triangle, and a rectangle.
2. On one shape the children place several drops of watercolor with a brush.
3. The children stand directly over the pool of watercolor, blow directly through the straw and splatter the paint. They can use many colors to fill in the shape. Then they cut out the shape.
4. Repeat this procedure for each shape.

5. Attach a string to each shape and hang shapes from the ceiling. On the white side or back side, have the children print the name of the shape before attaching the string.

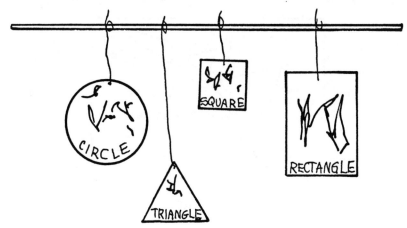

CONCEPT: Recognizing and Grouping Shapes by Various Relationships

---

GEOMETRIC DESIGNS

Materials: Construction paper
            Scissors
            Glue or paste

Procedure:

1. Cut out geometric shapes that are varied in size and color. Cut out some of the shapes into halves or quarters.

2. The children group a number of geometric shapes together until they form a picture.

3. When the children are satisfied with the arrangements, tell them to paste the shapes in place.

4. Try other designs. Use only triangles to make a monster.

5. Use squares and rectangles to make a man.

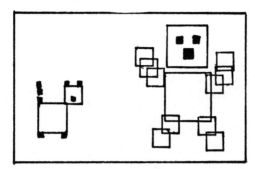

6. Use circles to make an animal.

THE SHAPE FAMILY

Materials: Construction paper cut into circles, triangles, squares, and
rectangles of various sizes
9-by-18 inch colored construction paper
Glue
5-by-7 inch brown envelope

Procedure:

1. Tell the children to design Cyril Circle, Tillie Triangle, Sigfred Square,
   and Harry Hexagon by using only those shapes called for each member
   of the family.

  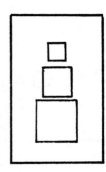 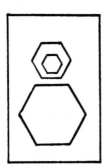

2. Attach, by gluing, a 5-by-7-inch brown envelope to the back of each
   family member.
3. Have the child look for the four basic shapes in old magazines and place
   them into the proper envelope for each member of the family.

COLORED CHALK RUBBINGS

Materials: Colored chalks
Hair spray or fixative
Typing paper

Procedure:

1. Have the children search out basic patterns on surfaces that use a basic
   shape as a motif. Lay white typing paper over the surface and rub gently
   with chalk to reproduce a pattern. Have the children find as many
   patterns as possible. Some groups could look for only rectangular
   shapes, some for only circular shapes, etc.

2. Lightly spray rubbings with hair spray of fixative to prevent smearing.

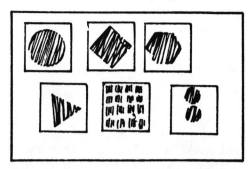

3. Have the children identify the basic shape used in the motif.

ENVIRONMENTAL BOX SCULPTURES

Materials: Old magazines
Cardboard grocery box
Glue
Scissors

Procedure:

1. Have each child make a collage by covering one cardboard box per child. Instruct them in covering each of the surfaces (sides) with pictures they cut from magazines that emphasize one shape for each side.

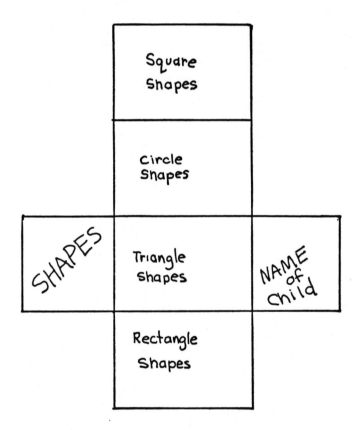

2. Cut construction paper letters for sides A and B. On side A, have the child cut out his or her name and glue the letters on the side. On side B, cut out the word SHAPES from construction paper.

3. Arrange the collage boxes into a large sculpture by stacking them like building blocks into a pleasing arrangement.

TISSUE-PAPER WINDOW DECORATIONS

Materials: Wax paper
Liquid starch
Brush
Tape
Various shapes cut from multicolored tissue paper

Procedure:

1. Arrange various geometric shapes into an interesting composition on a sheet of wax paper. Overlap some shapes. Be sure all shapes are touching one another.

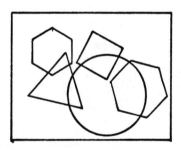

2. Coat the tissue-paper shapes with liquid starch by dabbing the solution onto the shapes with a brush.

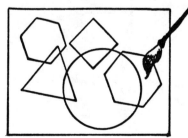

3. Allow to dry thoroughly. When dried, peel shapes away from wax paper and tape to a window. Sunshine will brighten the window decorations.

SHAPE DANGLES

Materials: Multicolored felt pieces cut into basic shapes
String
Glue
Displaying tree

Procedure:

1. From multicolored felt pieces, cut squares, circles, triangles, and rectangles into four sizes.

2. Glue two of the larger shapes back to back. Inside larger shape, glue smaller shapes.

3. Attach string at top and hang on classroom displaying tree.

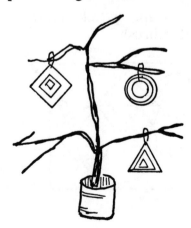

CYLINDRICAL CREATURES

Materials: Multicolored construction paper
Scissors
Glue
Stapler

Procedure:

1. Fold a large sheet of construction paper vertically at various intervals. Starting with the first fold, cut out little shapes.

2. The cutout design can then be placed over a contrasting sheet of construction paper of the same size that has been shaped into a cylinder.

3. Staple ends together.

Lantern

Cylindrical people

Cylindrical masks

Cylindrical creatures

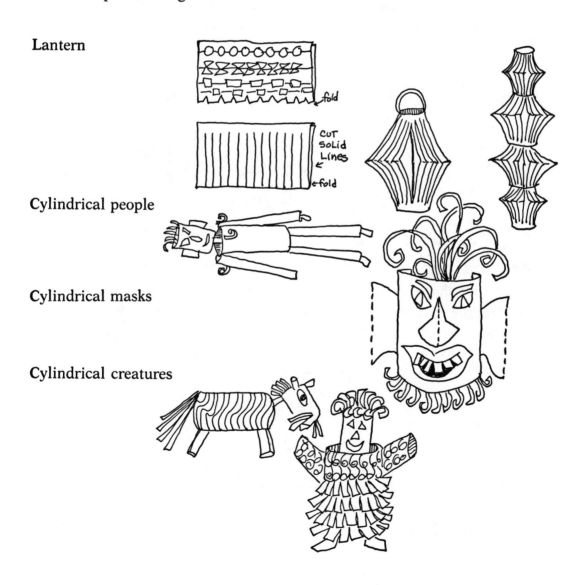

CONCEPT: Understanding and Reproducing Common Polygons

CLOSED AND OPEN SHAPE TREE

Materials: A set of ten open and closed shape worksheets* reproduced on colored construction paper
Tacks

Procedure:

1. Make a tree diagram on a large bulletin board.

2. Cut out shape sections along dotted line. (See pages 143-152.)

3. Have the children tack the shapes on the proper branch of the shape tree.

4. Fill in the trees so that sections appear as leaves on the trunks. Children may want to decorate closed shapes before placing them on the tree trunk.

*The worksheet material is reprinted by permission from *Unit 21, Angles and Shapes: Student Manual*, Minnesota Mathematics and Science Teaching Project (MINNEMAST), a grant from the National Foundation, University of Minnesota, 1970, 5th printing.

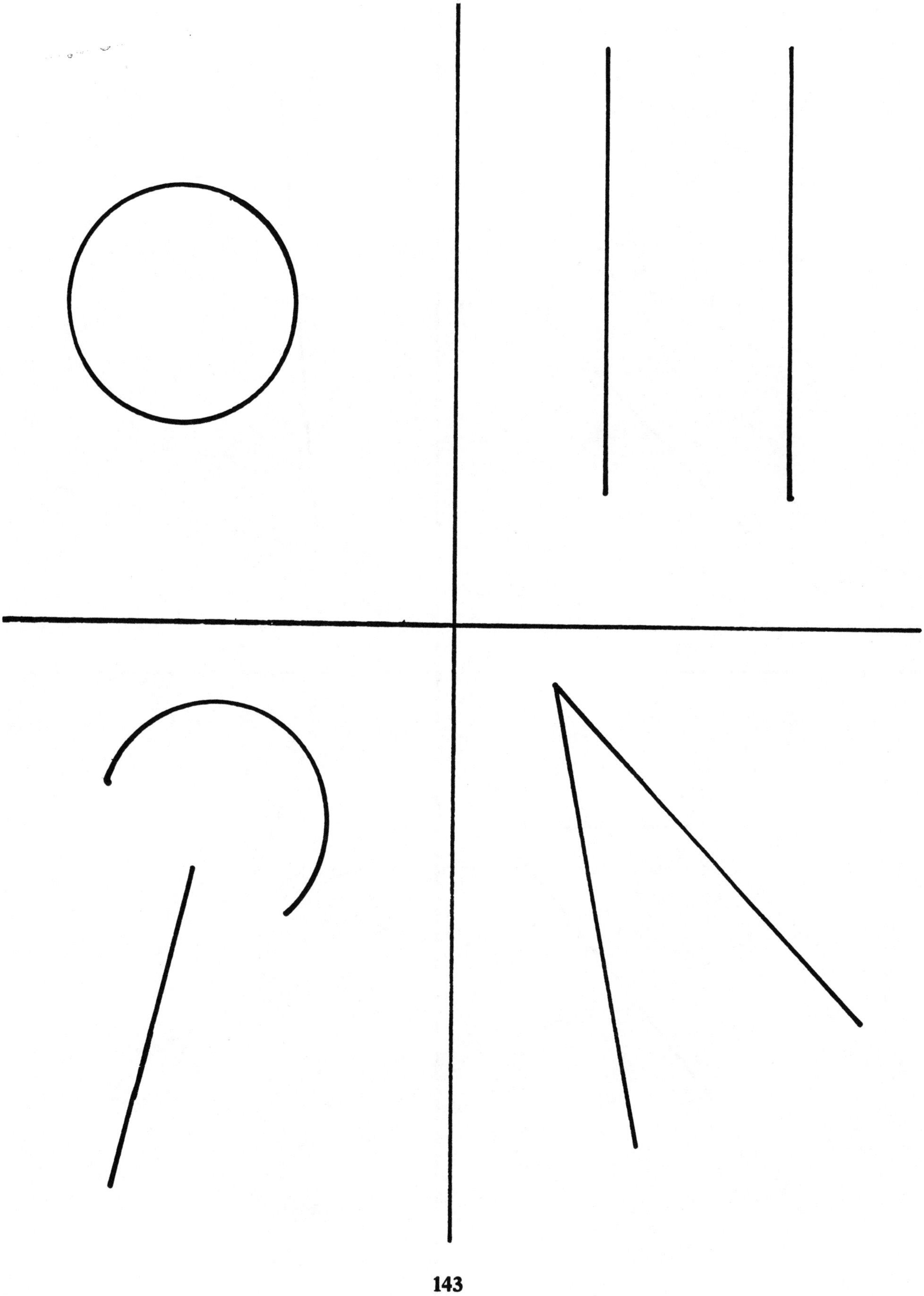

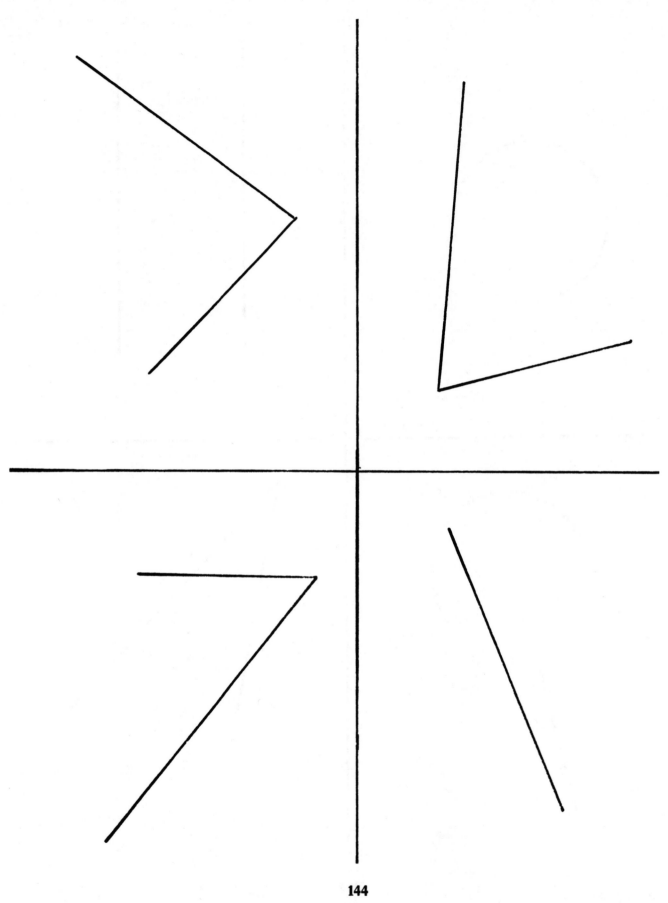

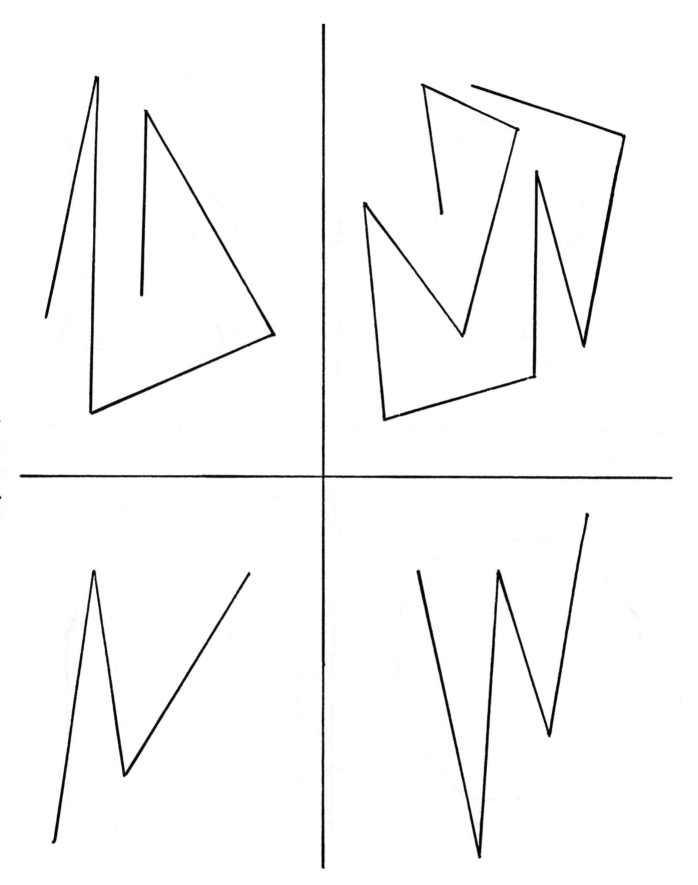

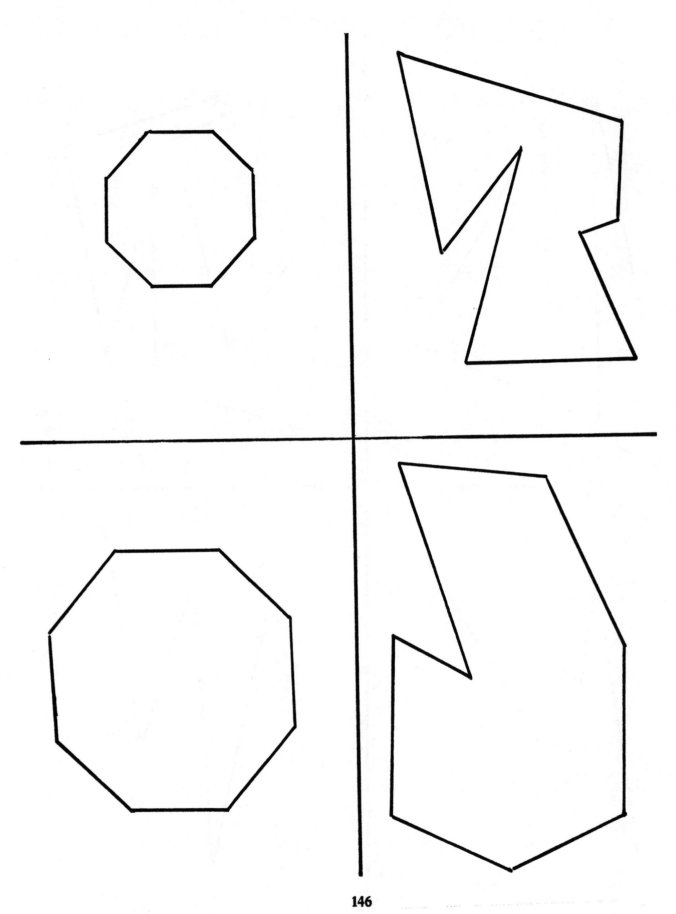

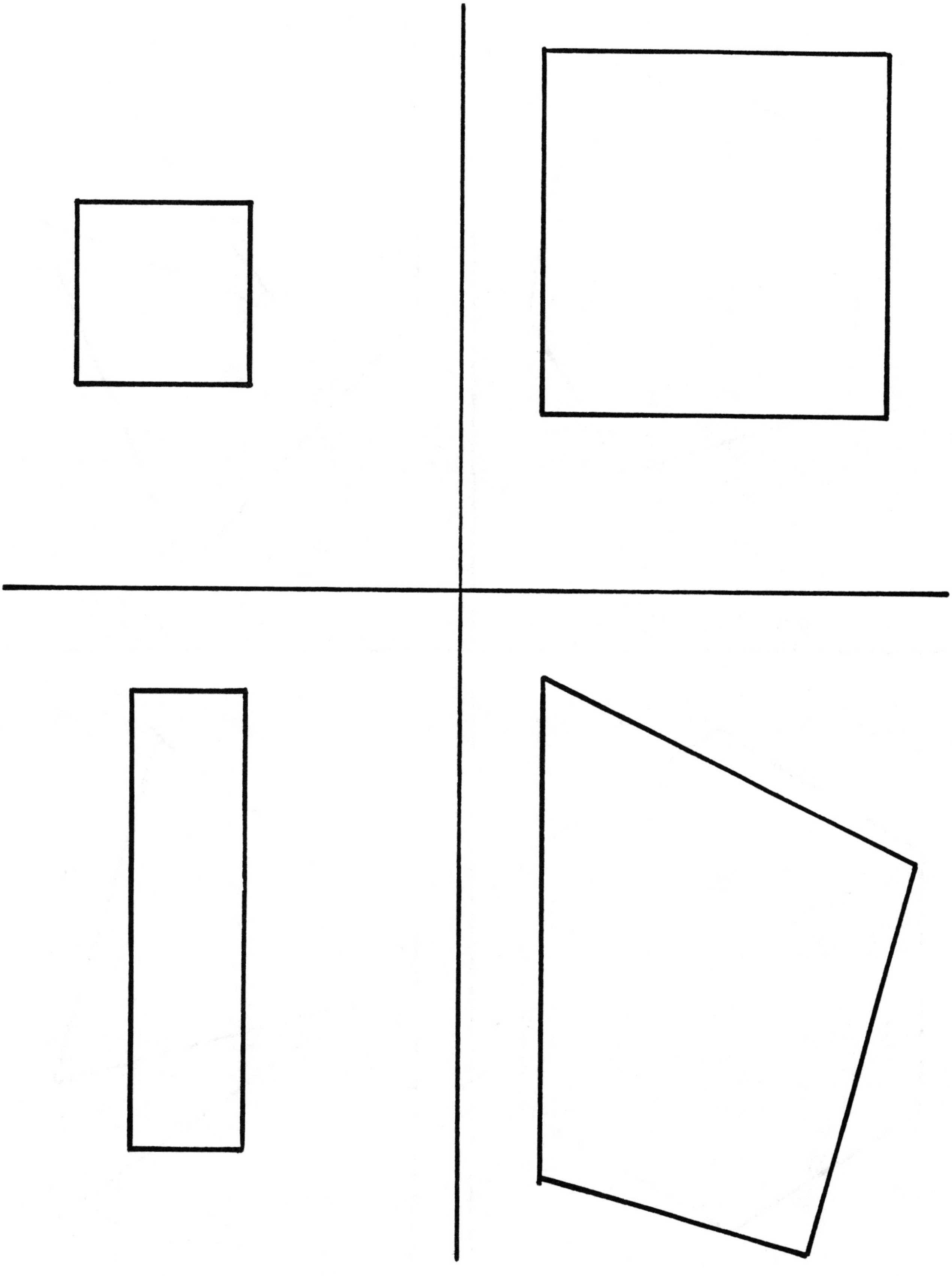

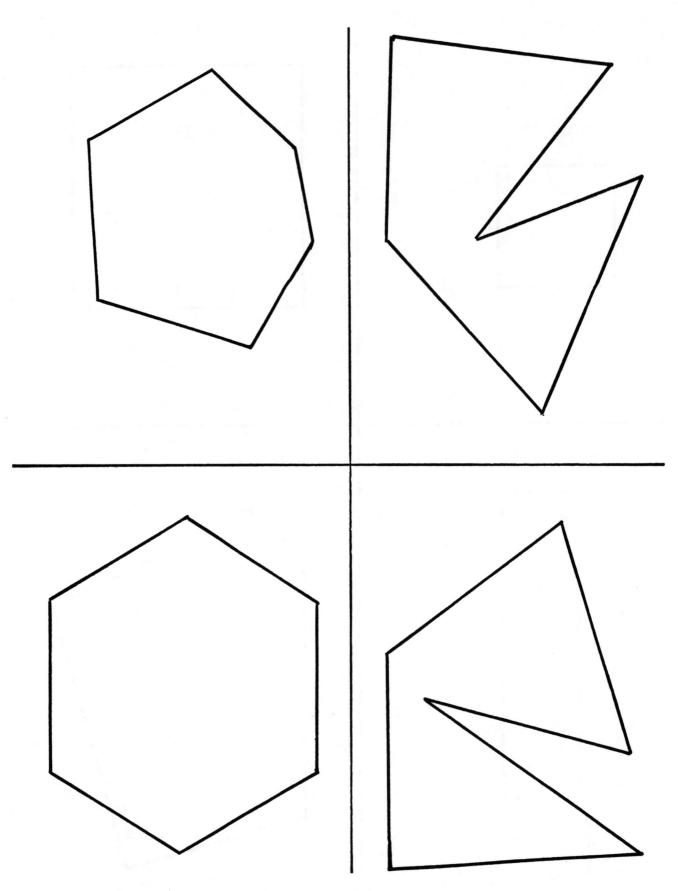

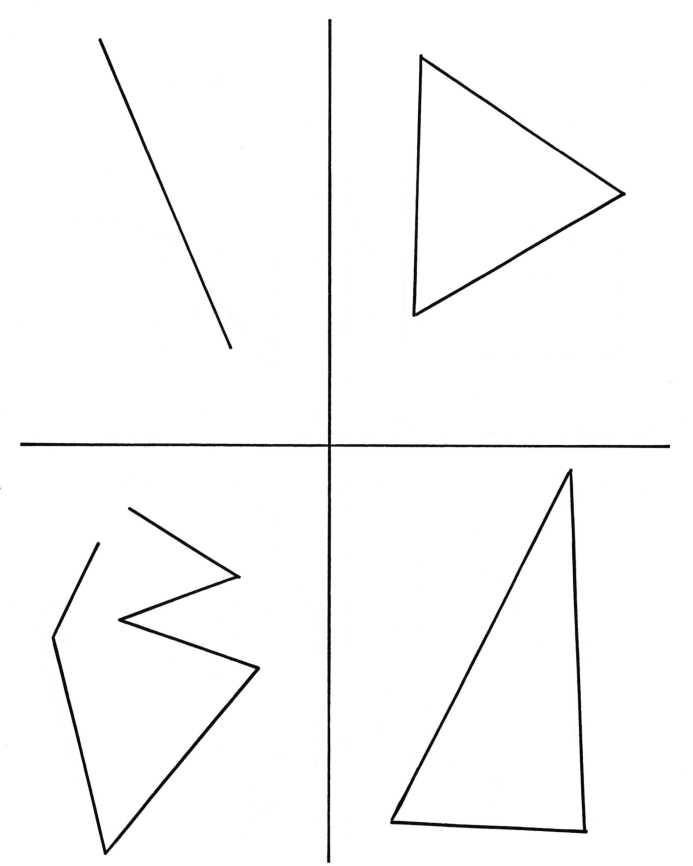

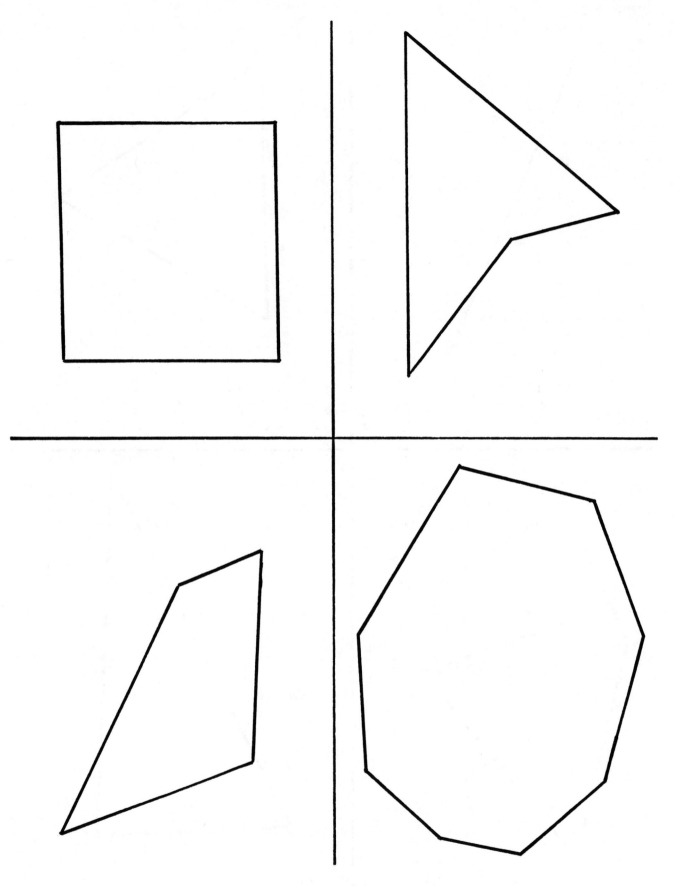

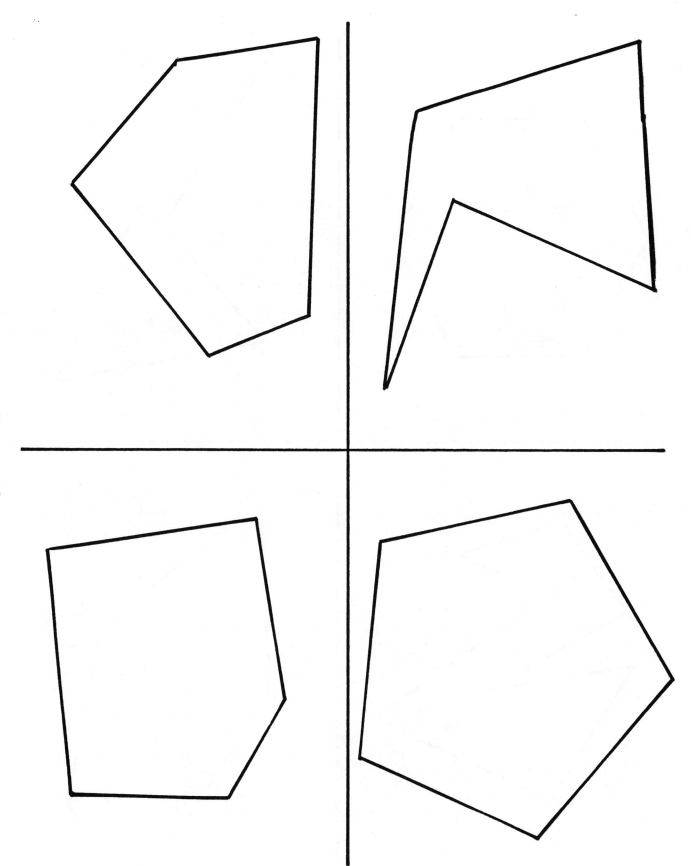

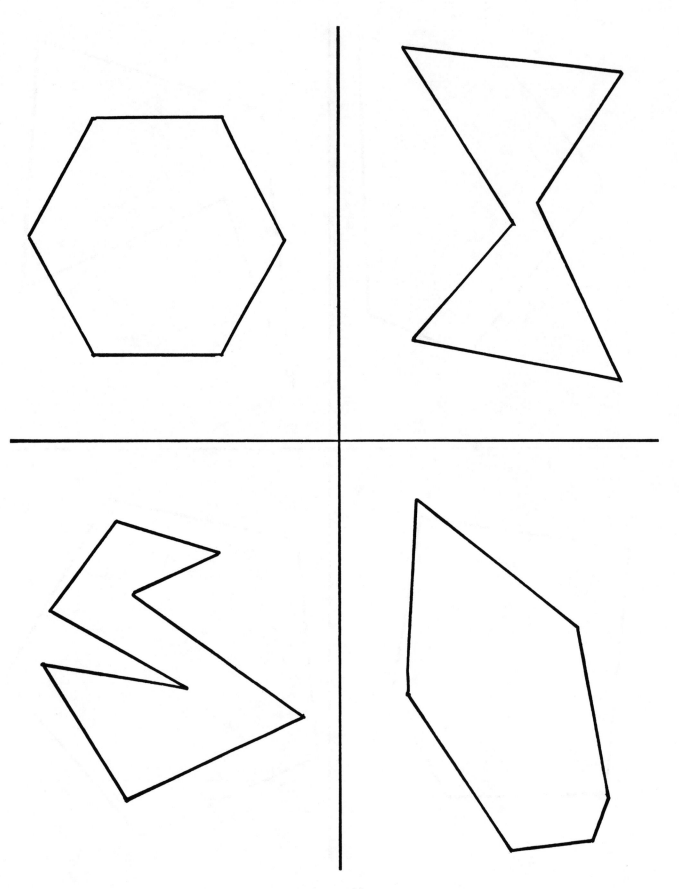

POLY-POLYGONS

Materials: Four worksheets (as provided)
Patterns
Magic markers
Glue
Scissors

Procedure:

1. Provide a pattern of one of the polygons (see pages 154-157) reproduced on white drawing paper for each child. Have each child decorate the pattern using magic markers. It is suggested that the child decide on a basic motif for one region and reproduce that same motif on all the sides.

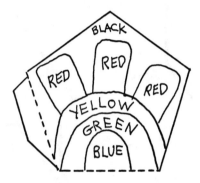

2. Cut and assemble polygon.

3. Display decorated polygons by making a large mobile. Allow the children to solve the problem of hanging shapes from a large dowel. Clothes hanger can be used to display mobile.

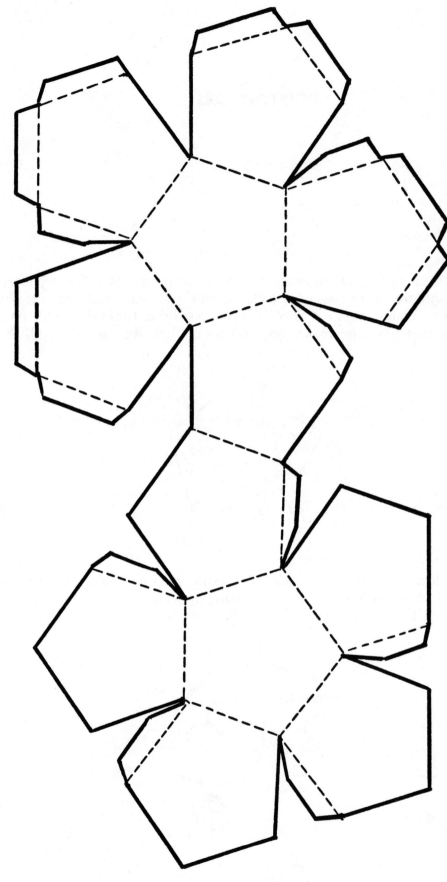

DODECAHEDRON

154

HEXAHEDRON

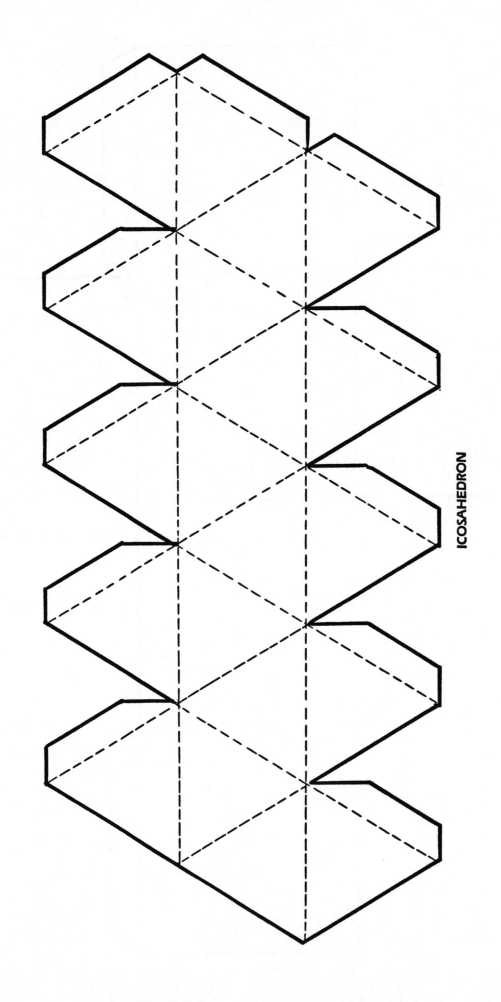

ICOSAHEDRON

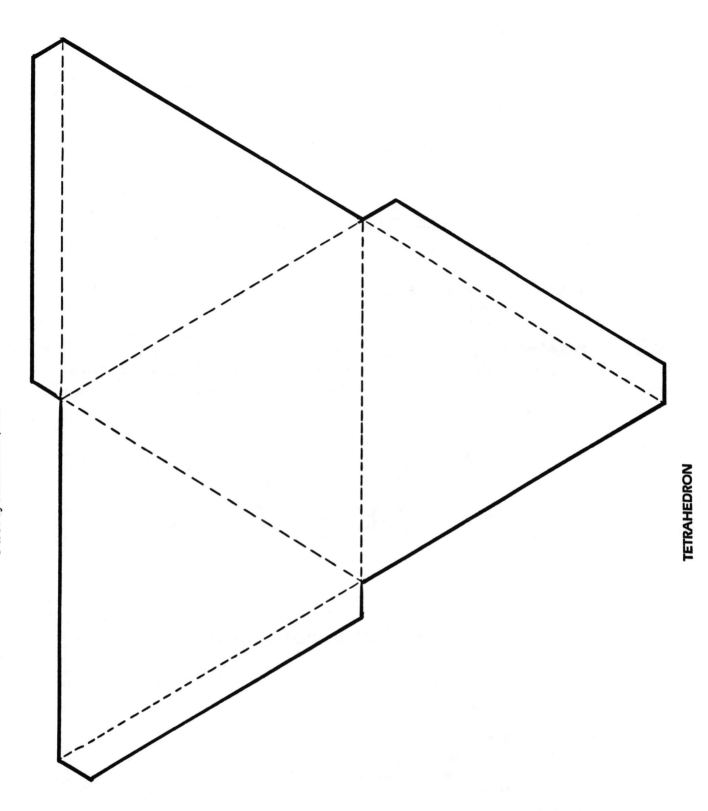

TETRAHEDRON

157

CONCEPT: Understanding, Reproducing, and Constructing Geometric Articles

MAKING DRAGONS AND CASTLES

Materials: Construction paper
Scissors
Glue

Procedure:

1. Follow the directions from previous lessons for making various shapes.
2. Make a dragon and a castle by using all of the shapes. Here is one example of a dragon.

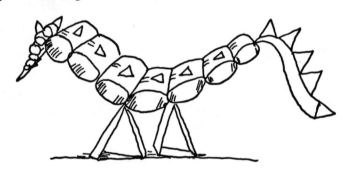

WAX-PAPER WINDOW DESIGNS

Materials: Crayons
Wax paper
Iron
Newspaper
Knife or sharp object for shaving
Thread

Procedure:

1. On a sheet of wax paper, shave various colors of crayon. (CAUTION: Allow the children to use the sharp object only under teacher supervision.)

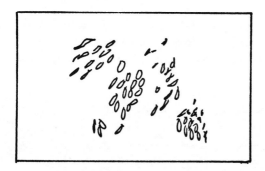

2. Cover crayon shavings with second piece of wax paper. Cover both pieces of wax paper with newspaper and press with warm iron. (CAUTION: The iron should be used only under teacher supervision.)

3. Cut basic Euclidean shapes from wax paper, insert thread, and hang shapes in a window for decorations.

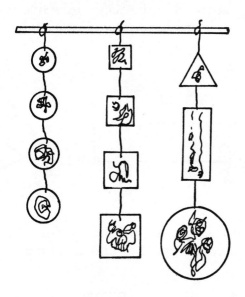

SHAPES 'N SCAPES

Materials: Construction paper
Scissors
Glue

Procedure:

1. Decide on a shape (triangle, square, rectangle, cylinder) with which a child will work. Do not mix shapes.

2. Cut construction paper into strips 2 inches wide and approximately 8 inches long. If the children choose to work with triangles, fold the paper into four folds as shown. Cut off excess paper not needed for four folds.

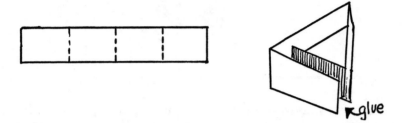

3. Overlap one fold and glue it to the side. Make as many triangles as the children wish. The children may want to make some triangles larger or smaller and they may want to make triangles of various colors.

4. If squares are chosen, fold the paper over five times and glue the last piece so that it overlaps to the side. Cut off excess paper not used after five folds.

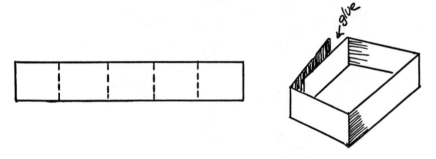

5. Make a sculpture using one of the shapes. Glue the pieces together in any pattern desired. Encourage the children to make a sculpture from each shape.

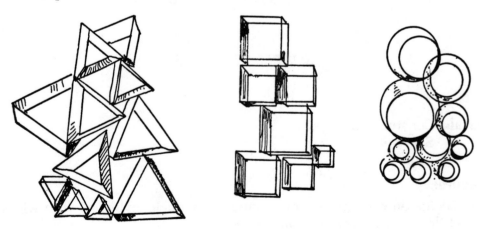

CONCEPT: Computing Perimeter and Area in Standard Units

PENTOMINO GAME

Materials: Pentomino game board (see page 162)
Set of Pentomino game pieces (see page 163)
Crayons

Procedure:

1. Color each set of Pentomino game pieces and board a different color.
2. Have the children try to cover the game board by solving the following problems:
   - Can you cover a 3-by-6-inch region? What is the area?
   - Can you cover a 5-by-8-inch region? What is the area? Are there any missing spaces?
   - Can you make a rectangular shape covering every square inch within the rectangular shape on the board?
   - Design problems for your friends to solve.

PENTOMINO GAME PIECES

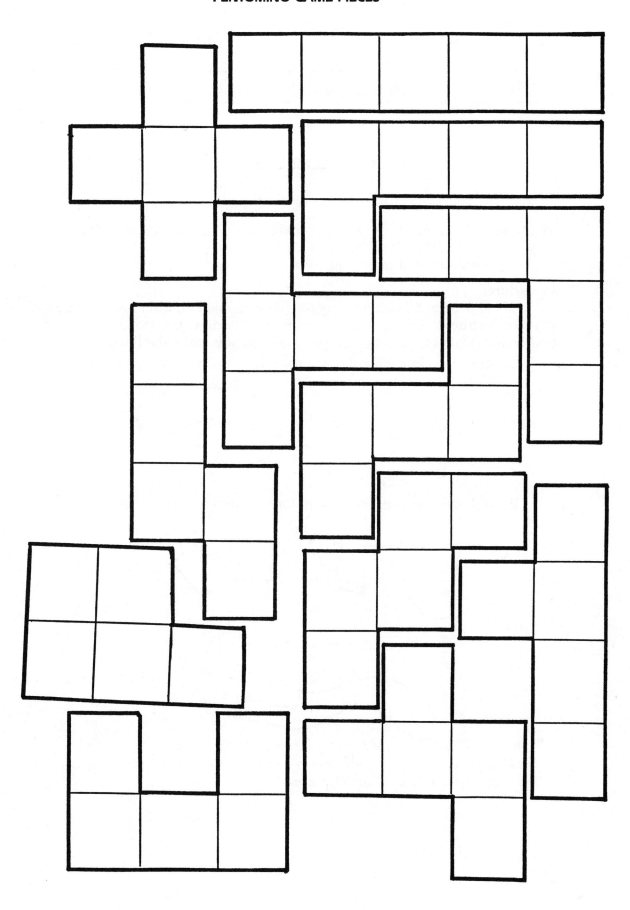

CONCEPT: Understanding Flexigon Strips

FLEXIGONS

Materials: Adding machine tape (approximately 15 inches for each child)
White glue or rubber cement
Multicolored magic markers

Procedure:
This may be a difficult activity for some primary children. It is suggested that you instruct the children in small group, providing material for each child, and demonstrate the step-by-step procedure as you make the flexigon.

1. Give each child a strip of white adding machine tape.

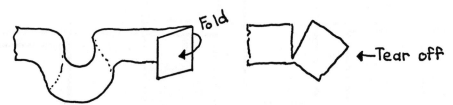

2. Fold one side over and tear to form a straight edge.

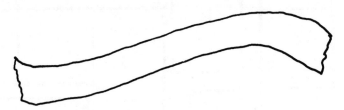

3. Crease tape at one end down center.

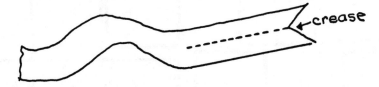

4. At crease, fold over right corner to form a diagonal line from tip of right corner to crease. Tear off piece.

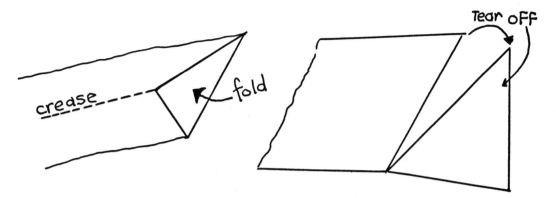

5. Fold right corner over to meet edge of paper. An equilateral triangle will appear.

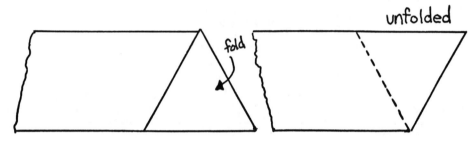

6. Fold over left corner again to meet upper edge. A second equilateral triangle will appear. Repeat procedure until ten equilateral triangles are creased into the paper tape. Tear off end.

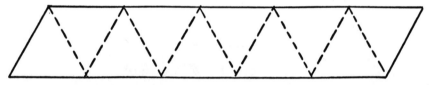

7. On both sides of tape, label with a pencil each equilateral region as follows:

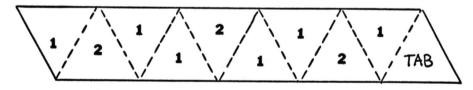

8. Holding tape horizontally, fold a "1" over first "2" on left side.

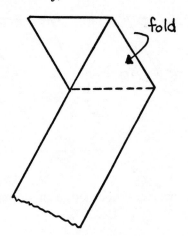

9. Turn counterclockwise, one rotation.

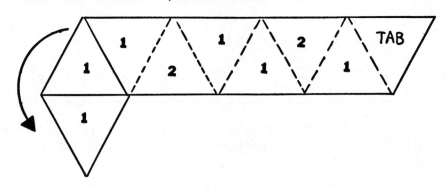

10. Fold "1" over second "2."

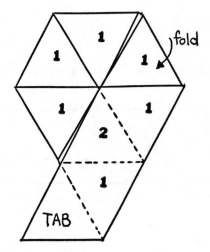

11. Turn counterclockwise one rotation.

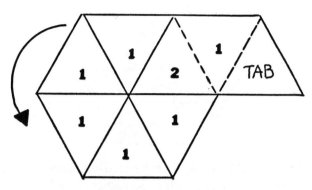

12. Fold "1" over third "2." Glue tab to first "1."

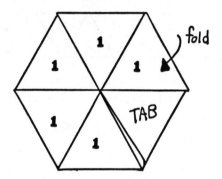

13. To flex, hold right side and press sides together to form something that looks like three butterflies joined together.

14. Points will fall open and a new surface will appear. Have the children decorate all three surfaces that can be obtained by flexing this particular flexigon.

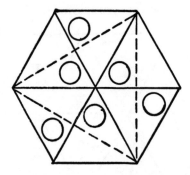

15. More complicated flexigons can be made using the same procedure by increasing the equilateral triangle regions to 19 and numbering each region as follows:

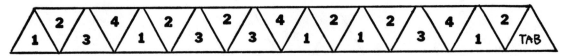

How many surfaces will this flexigon produce? Can the children figure out how to fold it? Hint: 2 folds over 1, 4 folds over 3, 4 folds over 2.

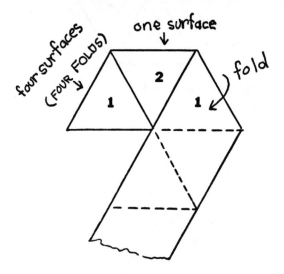

CONCEPT: Recognizing the Mobius Strip

MOBIUS STRIPS

Materials: Adding machine paper
　　　　　Tape
　　　　　Water colors

Procedure:

1. Paint a rainbow of colors on a piece of 18-inch adding machine paper. Paint both sides.

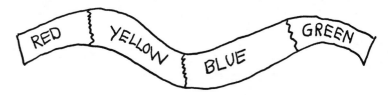

2. Twist paper once and tape together.

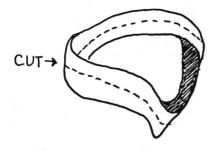

3. Cut paper once along length. What happens?
4. Cut again. What happens?

SYMMETRY AND PATTERNS

To the teacher

The activities in this section are designed to help children understand and reproduce three symmetry concepts. The symmetrical concepts are:

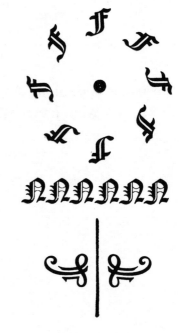

Rotational symmetry
(rotating a motif about a point)

Translational symmetry
(translating a motif along a straight line)

Bilateral symmetry
(reflecting a motif about a line)

170

Children may understand the separate symmetrical patterns more easily if certain terms are used interchangeably while presenting the activities. For example, you may want to use the word "turning" symmetry when teaching rotations, "repeating" symmetry for translations, and "mirror images" or "reflecting" symmetry for bilateral.

The creative activities are suggested ways children may explore symmetry through the free creation in pattern making. Encourage them to look for these symmetry patterns in things they may see around them; for example, in textiles, architectural designs, nature, animals, and plants. These objects may become a source of inspiration to the children and encourage originality in their art making.

CONCEPT: Finding and Completing Simple Patterns

CORNY PATTERNS

Materials: Popped popcorn
Needle and thread
Macaroni

Procedure:

1. Alternate popcorn and macaroni in a very simple pattern to begin the activity.

2. Tell the children they must put more on their chains than you have used.
3. Change the basic unit with each new necklace that is made.

CONCEPT: Understanding and Reproducing Rotational Symmetry

CHALK DESIGNS

Materials: Colored chalk
Crayons
Paper

Procedure:

1. With white chalk, draw a pattern on the board.

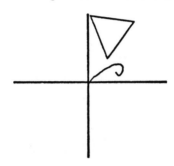

2. Ask the children to finish the pattern by retaining the rotational symmetry.

3. Have the children elaborate on the basic pattern by adding more details.

4. Draw another incomplete pattern with colored chalk. Again have the children complete and elaborate on the pattern. For example:

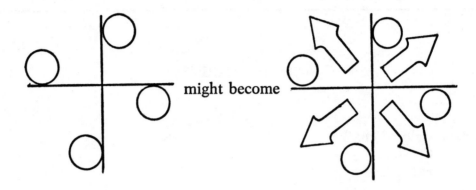

PAPER PATTERNS*

Materials: Scissors
White typing paper
Construction paper
Paste

Procedure:

1. Fold a sheet of typing paper into quarters.

2. Fold again along the diagonal.

3. Cut as shown to form a square.

4. Cut out design from folded paper. (If you wish, the children may draw a design before cutting.)

5. Unfold design and paste on colored construction paper.

---

*This material is reprinted by permission from *Unit 14, Exploring Symmetrical Patterns*, Minnesota Mathematics and Science Teaching Project (MINNEMAST), a grant from the National Science Foundation, University of Minnesota, 1971, 5th printing.

PAPER FLOWERS I*

Materials: Typing paper and thread
Scissors
Ruler
Pencil
String

Procedure:

1. Cut a sheet of typing paper to measure 6-by-11 inches. Fold pleats into the paper across the narrower dimensions. The pleats should be about ½ inch to 1 inch apart. Roll a pencil over the pleated paper to ensure deeply creased pleats.

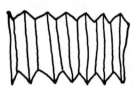

2. Fold pleated paper in half to crease.

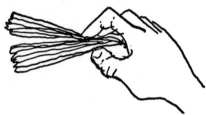

3. Tie securely at creased center with white thread and knot.

4. Fan ends and paste ends together to make a full circle.

*This material is reprinted by permission from *Unit 14, Exploring Symmetrical Patterns*, Minnesota Mathematics and Science Teaching Project (MINNEMAST), a grant from the National Science Foundation, University of Minnesota, 1971, 5th printing.

5. These make nice classroom decorations. Attach a thread to the top of each design and hang it from a string stretched across the classroom.

PAPER WHEELS*

Materials: Colored construction paper
Pencil
Scissors
Paste
Thread
String

1. Fold colored construction paper in half lengthwise. Crease the paper about 1 inch from the top.

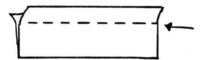

2. Mark off every ½ inch along the length of the fold. Cut at ½-inch marks as far as the crease. Do not cut to edge.

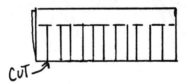

3. Overlap uncut edges and paste together.

4. Loop around and paste ends together.
5. Attach a thread to top of design and hang from a string running from one end of the classroom to the other.

*This material is reprinted by permission from *Unit 14, Exploring Symmetrical Patterns*, Minnesota Mathematics and Science Teaching Project (MINNEMAST), a grant from the National Science Foundation, University of Minnesota, 1971, 5th printing.

STARS*

Materials: Construction paper cut into 4-by-4-inch squares
Paste

Procedure:

1. Fold on dotted lines as indicated.
2. Fold forward on A and fold back on B.
3. Paste corner flaps of two squares together as shown in illustration. Continue pasting one square to the next; the last square is to be pasted to the first one.

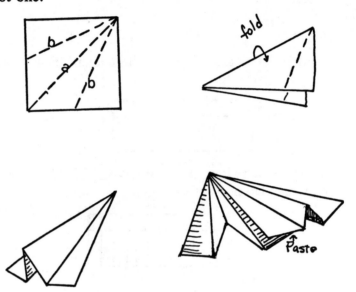

PAPER FLOWERS II**

Materials: Construction paper
Scissors
Glue

Procedure:

1. Fold a sheet of construction paper in half. Fold the sheet in half again, thus making a crease.

*This material is reprinted by permission from *Unit 14, Exploring Symmetrical Patterns*, Minnesota Mathematics and Science Teaching Project (MINNEMAST), a grant from the National Science Foundation, University of Minnesota, 1971, 5th printing.

**Ibid.

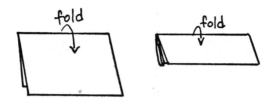

2. Open the second fold and make a tab by cutting from the center fold to the crease as shown in the diagram. Cut from center fold into crease, making strips ½-inch to ¾-inch wide.

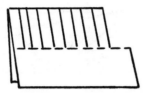

3. Glue the tab end to the other end, making a cylinder.

DECORATIVE SHAPES

Materials: Construction paper
         Scissors
         Glue
         Thread
         Tree branch

Procedure:

1. Cut basic shapes, either circles that measure 3 inches in diameter or 4-inch squares.

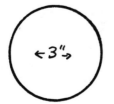

2. Fold the circles in half. Glue petals together to form a ball shape.

3. Fold squares along diagonal.

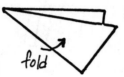

4. Glue petals together to form a pyramid shape.

5. Insert a thread at top and make a loop. Hang on a branch brought into the classroom.

ROSE WINDOW PATTERNS

Materials: Scissors
Pencil
12-by-18 inch white paper
Watercolors or crayons
Index card or tagboard piece approximately 5-by-7-inch long
Large pins

Procedure:

1. The children cut a design from a piece of heavy paper. Stick a pin through one end of the design and slip it into another larger sheet of paper.

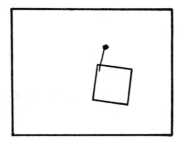

2. Next, trace the design. Turn the design a little and trace again.

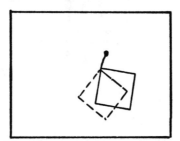

3. The children keep repeating this until they have completed a whole circle. When they are finished, there should be a pattern that shows rotational symmetry. Color or paint the design.

The design might look like this after it has been traced.

STICK WEAVING

Materials: Multicolored yarn
Popsicle sticks
Glue

Procedure:

1. The children glue two popsicle sticks together as shown.

2. Next, they wrap yarn around two parts of the sticks, spanning the space between. Tell them to avoid crossing strands over one another.

3. They repeat until sticks are covered. A knot is made at the end. Then they make a loop out of yarn and hang up on the wall. Variations can be made by using two dowels, coat hangers, or sturdy twigs.

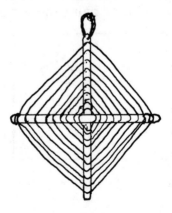

CONCEPT: Understanding and Reproducing Translational
Symmetry

PAPER DINNER MATS

Materials: Construction paper
Scissors

Procedure:

1. Tell the children to fold a sheet of 12-by-18-inch construction paper in half. Then they cut from folded edge to 1 inch from outer edge and unfold it. The children have a sheet with parallel slits that do not touch the edge of the paper.

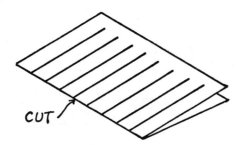

2. Next, the children cut construction paper of another color into 1-inch strips. They weave these through the slit sheets they have prepared.

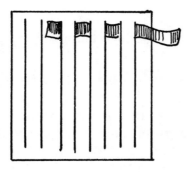

PAPER DESIGNS*

Materials: Construction paper or tissue paper, multicolored
Glue or spray glue

Procedure:

1. Show the children how to fold the paper into 2-inch pleats. They cut notches of different shapes in the folded edges. Then they unfold and paste on colored construction paper.

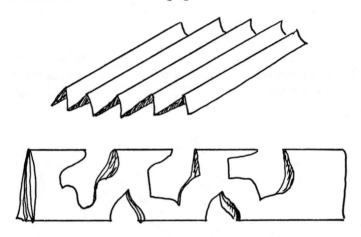

PRINT-MAKING DESIGNS

Materials: See each activity described below.

Procedure:

Any of the methods described below may be used for printing repeated patterns. Tempera may be brushed onto the printing surface, or water-base printer's ink may be rolled on with a brayer. If you use a brayer, squeeze a 3-inch ribbon of paint on a piece of glass and roll the brayer back and forth over it until it sounds sticky. Then roll the brayer over the printing surface. Newsprint or construction paper are best for printing, since they are more absorbent than other paper.

---

*This material is reprinted by permission from *Unit 14, Exploring Symmetrical Patterns*, Minnesota Mathematics and Science Teaching Project (MINNEMAST), a grant from the National Science Foundation, University of Minnesota, 1971, 5th printing.

1. *String Prints:* Wind a string around a piece of wood. Ink one side. Press inked string on newsprint to make a repeated pattern.

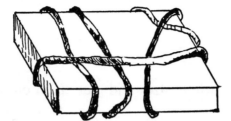

2. *Sponge Prints:* Ink a piece of sponge. Press the sponge on newsprint repeatedly.

3. *Soap-Eraser Prints:* Cut a design into one surface of a soap-eraser, ink it, and print.

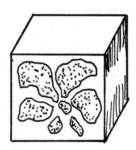

4. *Gadget Prints:* Ink kitchen gadgets, such as a potato masher, fork, or bottle cap, to make prints.

5. *Potato Prints:* Cut a potato in half. Have the children scratch a design on the cut surface with a pointed pencil. Watercolor or tempera should be applied to the potato surface with a brush, rather lightly, because the potato provides a good deal of moisture for the printing. Press the potato firmly on the paper.

LOOPS

Materials: Construction paper
Glue

Procedure:

1. Make loops of various sizes and glue them on construction paper in a repeating design.

STENCILS

Materials: Index cards
Crayons
Scissors
White construction paper

Procedure:

1. Cut a design from the center of a 3-by-5-inch index card. This design should *not* be symmetric. An unusual or odd shape will do. If a child cuts through the boundaries of the card, place a piece of tape over the cut.

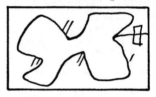

2. Place the card on construction paper. Use it as a stencil, rubbing crayon over the design to produce an image.

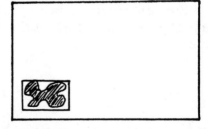

3. Show the children how to flip the stencil and repeat rubbing. They can make a repeated pattern by flipping the pattern over and over in a straight line. Have them fill in the whole sheet of paper by flipping or moving the stencil.

TIE-DYE PATTERNS

Materials: Plastic basins for at least three dyes (red, yellow, blue)
         Sticks for stirring
         Cloth (muslin, silk, or cotton)
         Plastic gloves to protect hands
         String
         Iron (CAUTION: To be used only by teacher.)

Procedure:

1. Prepare dyes in basins.

2. Fold cloth accordian style.

3. Press together and tightly tie cloth with string at various sections.

4. Dip one section into dye and allow cloth to absorb it for a few seconds.

5. Begin with yellow or lighter dye first, then proceed to darker dyes. When finished dying, untie string and open cloth. Hand to dry and iron.

SEED NECKLACES

Materials: Dried seeds (beans, watermelon, pumpkin, corn, etc.)
Cotton thread (heavy gauge) or nylon fishing line
Macaroni shells
Needle

Procedure:

1. Select a sequence to be a unit; for example, two corn, three watermelon, one lima bean, one macaroni.

2. Thread seeds and macaroni onto thread. Repeat unit.

3. Seeds can be softened in cold water and macaroni can be softened in warm water.

CONCEPT: Understanding and Reproducing Bilateral Symmetry

CONSTRUCTION PAPER DESIGNS

Materials: 12-by-18 inches and 9-by-12-inch multicolored construction paper
Glue
Scissors

Procedure:

1. Have the children cut out two or three shapes from the 12-inch edge of a sheet of 9-by-12-inch colored construction paper. Make sure the cuts are on the 12-inch edge, not the 9-inch edge.

2. Tell them to put the shapes aside and glue the sheet down on a 12-by-18-inch sheet of contrasting color.

3. Next the children take the cutout shapes and paste them down on the opposite side of the line of symmetry in a flipped position. Good color combinations are blue paper on yellow, green on orange, or black on white.

STAND-UP ANIMALS*

Materials: Construction paper
Crayons
Scissors
Glue

Procedure:
1. Fold a sheet of paper in half.
2. Draw an animal in such a way the the top of the drawing coincides with the folded edge. Color the drawing.
3. Cut through both layers of the drawing, turn over, and color the other half of the animal.
4. Glue the two layers of the head together. When the glue is dry, the legs can be spread so that the animal will stand. The children can make a farm, a circus, or a zoo with these animals.

VALENTINE CREATURES**

Materials: Red and white construction paper
Glue
Scissors

Procedure:
1. Cut out hearts of various sizes from the red and white construction paper.

*This material is reprinted by permission from *Unit 14, Exploring Symmetrical Patterns*, Minnesota Mathematics and Science Teaching Project (MINNEMAST), a grant from the National Science Foundation, University of Minnesota, 1971, 5th printing.
**Ibid.

2. Fold a large heart down the middle for the body. Fold smaller hearts in similar fashion for other body parts.

3. Glue the two halves of the head together, catching a little of the body between the layers so that the creature will stand.

4. To make other features, use smaller hearts pasted on in a bilateral symmetric pattern.

BRAYER PRINTS

Materials: Brayer
Cookie sheet
Newspaper
Newsprint
Leaves, bark, etc.
Tempera paint
Optional: wooden spoon

Procedure:

1. Help the children find natural symmetric objects. Leaves, grasses, and weeds usually illustrate bilateral symmetry. Bark often shows repeating patterns.

2. Squeeze a 3-inch ribbon of paint in the cookie sheet and roll the brayer back and forth over it until the brayer is smoothly coated with paint and sounds sticky. Lay the object on a piece of newspaper, and with the brayer, ink the surface. Do *not* apply so much ink that the spaces are filled in.

3. Lay the inked object face down on clean newsprint or construction paper and press down with either a clean brayer, your fingers, or the back of a wooden spoon. Children often find it easiest to use their fingers.

HANGING DECORATIONS

Materials: Construction paper
Thread
Sticks
Coat hanger
Scissors

Procedure:

1. Fold construction paper in half and draw half a bird or butterfly, using the center fold as the line that divides the animal.
2. Cut through both layers.
3. Suspend the animal by a thread through its center and tie to a rod of doweling or a wire coat hanger. Mobiles may be made of several dowels and many suspended paper figures.

LEAF RUBBINGS

Materials: Newsprint
Crayons or charcoal
Collected leaves

Procedure:

1. Help the children find leaves and weeds exhibiting bilateral symmetry. Place the newsprint over the object and rub the charcoal or crayon firmly over the paper. Mount the rubbings on a piece of construction paper for display.

2. The same technique can be used for other types of symmetry. A brick wall and tile floor are good examples of translational symmetry. Place newsprint over the object and rub with a crayon or charcoal.

CURVE STITCHING

Materials: 9-by-9-inch tagboard
Yarn
Yarn needles

Procedure:

1. Mark off the tagboard into quarters. Mark along lines at 1-inch intervals. Label X-axis with letters and Y-axis with numbers.

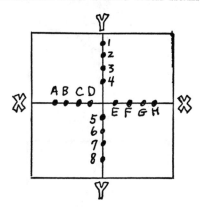

2. Before starting the stitching, the children should poke a hole through the tagboard with the yarn needle at each marked point. Begin stitching from the back of the tagboard. Knot yarn, then pull needle and yarn through 1. Insert in E and come up through F. Demonstrate the stitching to the children and have them follow you step by step.

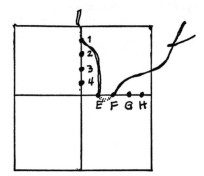

3. Continue sewing curve by stitching from F, over to 2, up through 3, and over to G, up through H, and over to 4.

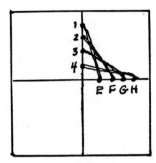

4. Those children who did not have trouble with this may want to do another section. Number along the lines as shown. Then stitch next curve as follows: H to 5, 6 to G, F to 7, 8 to E.

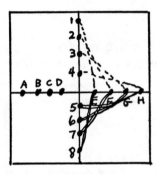

5. Sew each quarter until pattern is made.

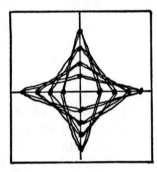

6. Children who grasp the one-to-one correspondence in this activity may want to try curve stitching other shapes, such as a triangle or a hexagon. They may use different colored yarns in a symmetric color pattern.

FINISH THE PATTERN

Materials: ½-inch or 1-inch grid paper
Crayons

Procedure:

1. Draw a line down the center of the grid paper shown on page 196. Outline a pattern to the left of the line. Have a friend make the pattern bilaterally symmetric on the right side.

STRING PATTERNS

Materials: 12-inch string
White paper
Paint or ink
Big heavy book

Procedure:

1. Fold a sheet of white paper in half.
2. Dip string in tempera paint. Coat thoroughly.
3. Place paint-soaked string on one side of the paper and fold over with other side. Be sure to make an interesting pattern with the string on the paper and leave each end hanging out.

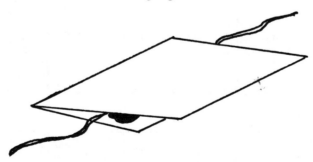

4. Cover folded paper and string with heavy book. Gently lift off the string at one end. Open paper for bilaterally symmetrical pattern.

NIP BUGS

Materials: Scissors
Glue
Colored paper
Two tacks
Snap-on clothespins

Procedure:

1. Push tacks into clothespins, making two eyes.

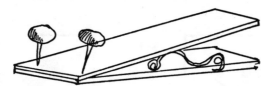

2. Cut out some paper legs and glue them on the reverse side of the clothespin.

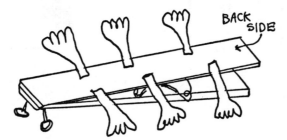

3. Cut out some wings and a tail. Color the wings with dots. Glue them to the clothespin.

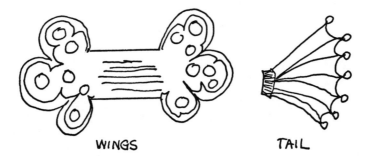

WINGS   TAIL

BLOTCH NOTCHES

Materials: 12-by-18-inch white paper
Tempera paint or ink
Brush

Procedure:

1. Fold paper in half to crease.

2. On right side of crease, drop various blotches of color.

3. Fold paper over blotches, press firmly over folded paper, and open for bilateral design.

 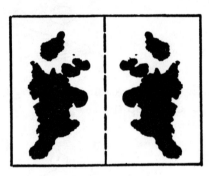

CONCEPT: Understanding and Reproducing Symmetrical Patterns: Bilateral, Rotational, and Asymmetrical

PAPER STRIP SCULPTURES

Materials: Multicolored paper strips
Construction paper
Paste
Staples
Scissors

Procedure:

1. Make animals, figures, and patterns as shown. Attach strips together with paste, tape, or staples.

PAPER STRIP HATS

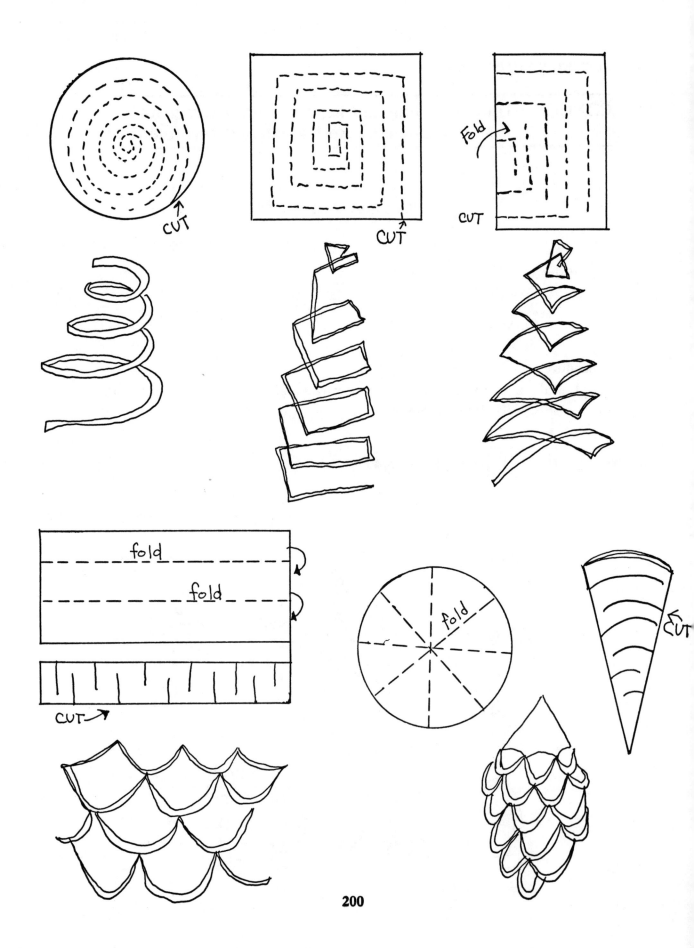

CUT

CUT

Fold

CUT

fold

fold

fold

CUT

CUT

200

Section 10
MONEY

To the teacher

The activities on money are organized to teach children a stated value up to:

a. 25 cents
b. 50 cents
c. 1 dollar
d. Recognizing 1 cent through 1 dollar

You may need to prepare materials for the children when using these activities. It is suggested that a rubber coin stamp be used in order to reproduce a coin motif on index cards or paper to make a deck of cards so that children recognize and identify a specific value of a coin by its image.

Play money can be designed by you or by the children and be reproduced on a ditto.

CONCEPT: Interchanging Coins of Stated Value Up to 25 Cents

SAVING FOR FUN

Materials: Play money (1 cent, 5 cents, 10 cents, and 25 cents)
Old games, toys, etc.
Small boxes
Construction paper
Glue
Crayons

Procedure:

1. Have the children decorate and design a bank from a small box to hold money earned each day.

2. Set up a store and a reward system for work finished or good behavior. Begin by giving each child 25 cents in play money. A child can save the earned money or spend it. Some may want to earn more. Use the play money as reinforcers and rewards for desired behavior. When a child saves enough money, allow him or her to purchase something from the classroom store.

3. Since this is a very intricate activity, you will have to decide how to set up the store, who will manage it, when it will be open for business, and how the money will be recorded. Children can be taught to keep the store's books of what is purchased and what is not.

MONEY FOR YOUR WORDS

Materials: Paper
Pencil
Chart

Procedure:

1. Make a chart showing the following values for each letter of the alphabet:

A = 1¢	G = 6¢	N = 5¢	T = 5¢
B = 7¢	H = 4¢	O = 7¢	U = 3¢
C = 3¢	I = 8¢	P = 1¢	V = 6¢
D = 2¢	J = 1¢	Q = 6¢	W = 2¢
E = 5¢	K = 8¢	R = 4¢	X = 5¢
F = 9¢	L = 3¢	S = 2¢	Y = 1¢
	M = 9¢		Z = 10¢

2. Use the chart to find the value for the following activity:

   a. Write out this week's spelling words. Figure out the value of each word. Which word on the list has the most value? The least value?
   Example:

   H   O   U   S   E
   4¢ + 7¢ + 3¢ + 2¢ + 5¢ = 21¢

   b. Having children work in groups of two, ask them to think of a word that has the same number of letters in it. Write it down. Have them compare values. Who has the word with the most value?

   c. Find the value of the following:
   Child's first name _____
   Child's last name _____
   School's name _____
   City in which the child lives _____
   State _____
   Teacher's name _____
   Pet's name _____
   Friend's name _____

3. Change the values of the letters in the alphabet periodically in order to make the activities more challenging.

TIC-TAC-TOE

Materials: Deck of problem cards
Two different colored crayons
Paper
Index cards

Procedure:

1. Make up a deck of problem cards with money word problems. Place the problem on one side of the card and the answer on the reverse side of the card.

2. Have one of two children pull a card and work out the problem. If the child is correct, he or she places a cent sign in the Tic-Tac-Toe grid, using a color representing himself or herself.

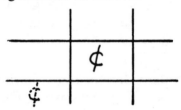

3. Here are sample card problems and combinations.

MONEY DOMINOES

Materials: Domino cards
Scissors

Procedure:

1. Make up the following set of domino cards on a ditto sheet. Children then cut out dominoes.

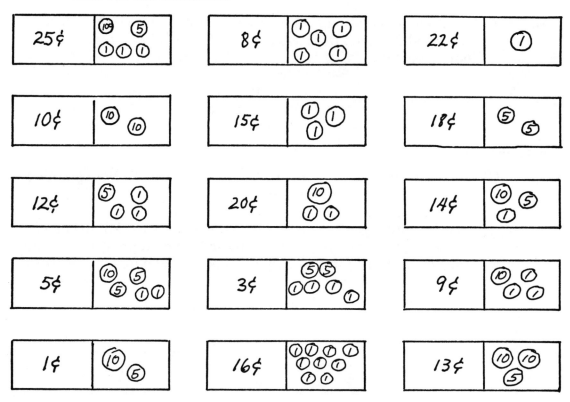

2. Have the children match the parts of equal value.

CONCEPT: Interchanging Coins of Stated Value
Up to 50 Cents

CAN YOU BUY IT?
(a game for two players)

Materials: Set of index cards stamped with coin motif: 1 cent, 5 cents, 10 cents, and 25 cents. Deck should include the following number of individual cards:

> 1¢—10 cards
> 5¢—10 cards
> 10¢—10 cards
> 25¢— 5 cards

Procedure:

1. Provide a gameboard (found on page 207) for each child. You may want to change the gameboard periodically.

2. Instruct the children with the following directions:

> Shuffle the cards. Place them face down. Draw a card. If the money on the card adds up to enough to buy an item on your board, put the card or cards next to the item. If it does not add up to the correct amount, save the card until the next draw. Take turns. The first one to buy all the items wins.

Will You Buy It?

29¢		10¢
50¢		12¢
49¢		16¢
30¢		25¢
39¢		46¢
40¢		35¢

THREE-CARD MATCH GAME

Materials: Three decks of index cards made in the following manner:

Deck A	Deck B	Deck C
(25) (10) (5) (1) (1)	.42	Forty-Two cents
(25) (10) (5) (1) (1) (1)	.49	Forty-nine cents
(10) (10) (5)	.25	Twenty-five cents
(10) (5) (1)	.16	sixteen cents
(25) (25)	.50	Fifty cents
(10) (10) (10) (5)	.35	Thirty-five cents
etc.	etc.	etc.

Procedure:

1. Shuffle cards. Deal seven cards to each player. Place deck face down in center between players. Try to match cards to make a three-card set.
2. Each player checks his or her hand to see if he or she has a set. If so, he or she lays the cards face up for verification. If no cards match, the player draws a card from the deck. The player with the most sets wins.

CONCEPT: Interchanging Coins of Stated Value
Up to One Dollar

"SEVENTY-FIVE"
(a game for two players)

Materials: Three decks of index cards stamped with the following:

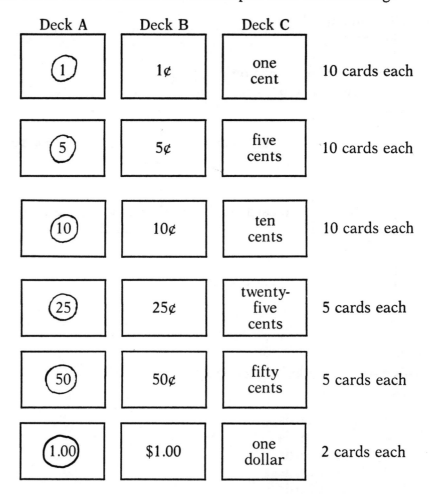

Deck A	Deck B	Deck C	
① 1	1¢	one cent	10 cards each
⑤ 5	5¢	five cents	10 cards each
⑩ 10	10¢	ten cents	10 cards each
㉕ 25	25¢	twenty-five cents	5 cards each
㊿ 50	50¢	fifty cents	5 cards each
(1.00)	$1.00	one dollar	2 cards each

Procedure:

1. Shuffle cards. Each player takes a card. A player continues to draw cards one at a time until the child comes as close to 75 cents as possible. The player who comes as close to 75 cents without going over, wins. (Note: This game can be played with other numbers: 50 cents, 25 cents, or 1 dollar.)

2. Variation: *War*—Divide the cards into two even piles. Each player draws two cards from the top of each pile. The sum value of each card is stated. The higher value wins and that player then keeps his or her cards. The loser returns the cards to the bottom of the pile. The player who runs out of cards loses. (Note: Ties are played out by adding cards from individual piles until one player breaks the tie with a higher card.)

MONEY RACEWAY GAME

Materials: Two to four players
Markers
1 die
Gameboard as shown on page 211
Teacher-made money with coin stamps on index cards.

| 1¢ | 40 cards each | | 25¢ | 15 cards each |

| 5¢ | 30 cards each | | 50¢ | 8 cards each |

| 10¢ | 20 cards each |

Procedure:

1. This game is similar to Monopoly.

2. Give each child:

> 5— 1 cent cards
> 4— 5 cent cards
> 3—10 cent cards
> 2—25 cent cards
> 1—50 cent cards

3. Players roll a die and move the number of spaces indicated on die. Each player must follow the directions in each cell. The first to reach the finish line wins.

4. Players pay to bank or receive from bank what is due.

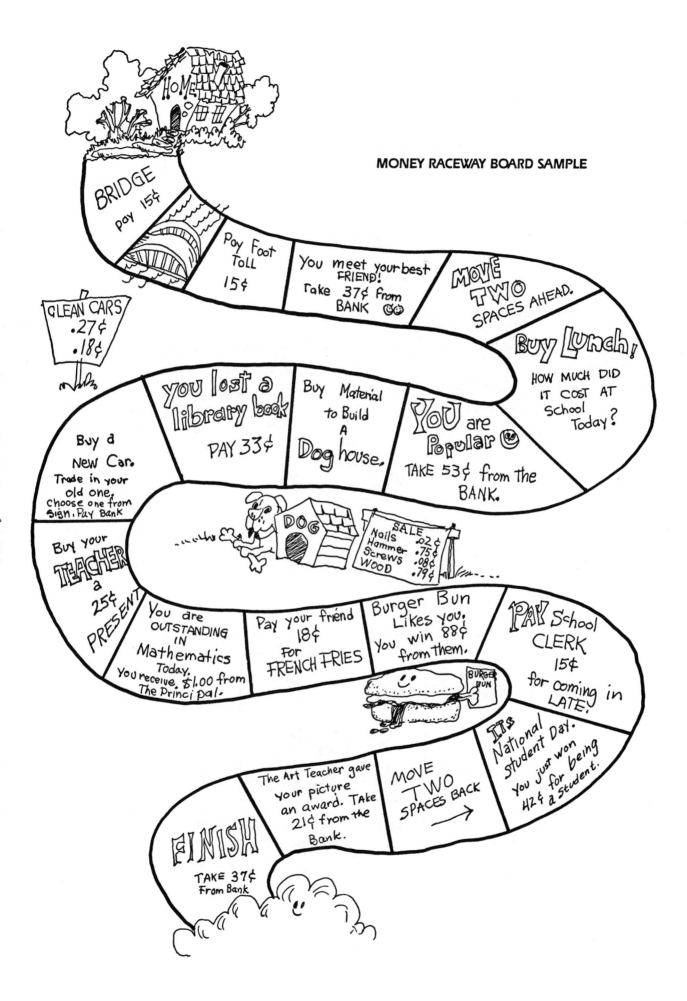

MONEY RACEWAY BOARD SAMPLE

CONCEPT: Recognizing and Identifying Coins
and Currency from One Cent to One Dollar

COIN PATTERNS

Materials: Onionskin typing paper
                  Soft lead pencils
                  Penny, nickel, dime, quarter (one set for each child)

Procedure:

1. Give each child a sheet of onionskin typing paper. Have the children make a rubbing using a soft lead pencil of a penny, nickel, dime, and quarter. Have them make as many pennies, dimes, nickels, and quarters as they wish on the sheet of paper.

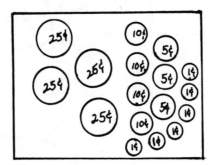

2. Have them add up how much is represented on the paper.

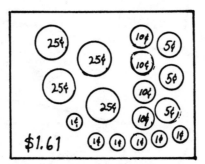

3. Make a design on the paper using the coins and rubbing over them. How much money was used to make the patterns?

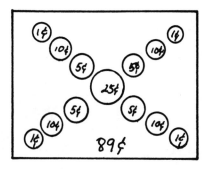

PRICING POWER

Materials: White paper

Crayons or pencils

Procedure:

1. Make some play money. Allow the children to design their own penny, nickel, dime, quarter, and dollar. Make five dollars' worth of play money and arrange as shown on the sheet below.

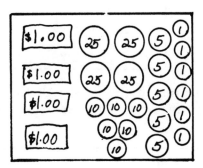

2. For homework, ask the children to go to the grocery or their favorite store and price an item or items they wish to purchase that is not over five dollars. The next day, have the children tell the prices and see how much of their play money they would need to purchase the items.

DOLL

CAN YOU MATCH THE AMOUNT?

Materials: Teacher-made cards with coin stamp—approximately 18 value
combinations
Two gameboards on ditto sheets

Procedure:

1. Using a coin stamp, make up a set of cards with various amounts
   stamped on the card.

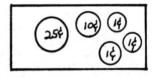

2. Have the children match the card wth the correct amounts on the
   gameboard or ditto sheet. The first student to fill up his or her
   gameboard wins.

98¢	52¢	37¢
31¢	$1.00	63¢
12¢	49¢	75¢

84¢	35¢	51¢
9¢	91¢	27¢
78¢	14¢	43¢

KNOWING YOUR COINS

Materials: White drawing paper
Newspaper with advertisements for groceries
Glue or paste
Scissors

Procedure:

1. Cut out pictures of various food items from the newspaper. Cut out prices along with item. Paste onto grid as shown. Ask children to write out which coins they would select to pay for each item.

JAM	40¢	2 DIMES 2 NICKELS 10 Pennies
CEREAL	$1.25	1 Dollar 1 Quarter
BUBBLE GUM	15¢	1 DIME 1 NICKEL

2. Make up a large chart with a value on it. How many combinations of coins will make the amount shown?

	40¢		
Quarters	1		
Dimes	1	4	2
Nickels	1		2
Pennies			

	50¢		
Quarters	1	1	
Dimes	2		5
Nickels	1	3	
Pennies		10	

	60¢		
Quarters	2	1	
Dimes	1	1	5
Nickels		3	2
Pennies		10	

3. On twenty blank cards, write a spending or an earning statement.

SPEND 3 DIMES	EARN 2 QUARTERS

Place the cards face down in a pile between two children. Give each student the same amount of money to begin the game. Three dollars might be a good amount. The children take turns drawing from the deck by adding or subtracting the amount of money listed on the card. Each child draws a total of five cards. The child with the greater amount of money remaining wins the game. Have the children check each other's arithmetic after each card is drawn. If a child makes an error in addition or subtraction, the other child wins the game.

Section 11

TIME

To the teacher

Teaching children the sense of time, how to tell time, and how to measure it is often a difficult task. Children seem to be egocentric responding to events happening in their lives. Often they have difficulty relating these events to a specific point in time.

Most of the activities in this section reinforce basic notions of time measurement: telling time to the nearest hour; using the terms "morning," "afternoon," and "evening"; and reading and identifying days of the week and days on a calendar.

One of the most creative activities is journal keeping. Each lesson is designed to stimulate creative and inventive thinking in the children and helps them record activities by the days of the week.

The activities in this section can actively involve both you and the children in their own creative expression. Have fun!

CONCEPT: Using Correctly the Terms "Morning," "Afternoon," and "Evening"

CATALOG CATEGORIES

Materials: Old shopping catalogs from major department stores
Scissors
Glue
Bulletin board

Procedure:

1. Divide a bulletin board into three sections labeled "morning," "afternoon," and "evening."

2. Have the children cut clothes and objects from the catalog and place them into the proper region. For example, what would someone wear in the morning? When would a toaster most likely be used? When would a bed most likely be used?

PAPERBAG MUNCHERS

Materials: Paperbags
Scissors
Old magazines
Construction paper
Glue

Procedure:

1. Have three paperbag puppets made by decorating the surface with construction paper. Label each bag as shown:

2. Cut a slit at the back of the mouth in the puppet.

3. Have the children cut out various pictures of food from magazines. Tell them to divide the cutouts into piles of food that would be eaten in the morning, food that would be eaten in the afternoon, and food that would be eaten in the evening.

4. Play a game and have the children feed the food into the proper puppet. You may hold up the afternoon puppet and ask for something from each child.

CONCEPT: Identifying the Days of the Week

CREATIVE WEEKLY JOURNAL

Materials: Spiral notebook
Crayons
Scissors
Magic markers

Procedure:

1. Have the children keep a weekly journal. On Monday instruct them to label two sheets or pages as follows:

Tell them to write a poem and illustrate the poem using both pages.

2. On Tuesday label the pages as before and assign them the problem of writing or printing their name in as many ways as they wish.

3. On Wednesday they can make a collage that tells all about themselves.

4. On Thursday the children can write new words to a popular song and illustrate the record cover on one of the pages.

5. On Friday the class can examine a bug, then draw it in detail on a page. Label the parts. Everyone can help write a make-believe story.

6. Saturday is a good day to design a food that no one ever thought of before. The children can give it a name and write a commercial for it.

7. On Sunday the children can make a floor plan of the inside of Snoopy's doghouse.

8. Continue this process until the journal is filled with creative ideas. Use some of the following creative starters. When the journal is finished, they can bring it home to their parents.

HINTS: JOURNAL IDEAS FOR DAILY ASSIGNMENTS

A. Musical Ideas:

1. LOUD AND SOFT—Cut out pictures from magazines to make a collage visualizing loud and soft. For example, Loud could be represented by fireworks, someone yelling, or heavy equipment. Soft could be shown by kittens sleeping, or a romantic picture using pastel colors. Some pictures may illustrate both loud and soft.

2. LOUD AND SOFT—After looking at comparisons of art with bright, bold, explosive colors (loud) and subtle, less intense colors (soft), paint a picture that is loud and a picture that is soft. Coordinate with listening to Mozart's *Surprise Symphony* and observing differences in dynamics.

3. FAST AND SLOW—Draw pictures of things that are fast and things that are slow. Listening: (Fast)—*Flight of the Bumblebee* by Rimsky-Korsakov. (Slow)—*You Light Up My Life* by Debbie Boone or *Dance of the Little Swans* from *Swan Lake* by Tchaikovsky.

4. FAST AND SLOW—Fold paper in thirds. Draw or paint slow-fast-slow sections to correlate with slow-fast-slow sections of Hap Palmer's *The Elephant.*

5. FAST AND SLOW—Paint an abstract of fast and slow while listening to music.

6. TEXTURE—This exercise emphasizes thick and thin. Make a collage picture of thick materials and thin materials. A music example of a thick texture is a full symphony orchestra. Music examples of thin texture include solo instruments and small ensembles. Using rhythm instru-

ments, improvise rhythmic patterns. Start with one instrument, add one more, add one more, etc., until a thick texture is achieved. Gradually take away instruments one at a time until a thin texture is achieved.

7. FEELINGS—Paint peaceful, tranquil, calm feelings; then paint stormy furious, angry feelings; then again paint peaceful, calm feelings. (Fold a large piece of paper into thirds as you do this.) Listen to Beethoven's *Sixth Symphony (Pastorale Symphony)*. The music begins quiet, peaceful, etc., then builds to the storm, then becomes peaceful and calm.

B. Kindergarten Suggestions:

Individual sheets are to be collected by you and assembled by the children.

1. Trace hands—The children draw something they like to do with their hands. This activity could be done with other body parts, for example, eyes, ears, etc.

2. Texture pictures of design—Have objects available for the children that are smooth, rough, soft, hard, etc. Make sure that the objects being used are ones that can easily be glued to the page of the journal.

3. Collage—The children work on the theme "All About Me." Pieces are cut from magazines.

4. Creative name writing—Tell the children to do something creative with their names (better at the second semester).

5. Drawing to music.

6. Ink Blot—Use tempera paints: fold paper in half, then have the children dictate to you what they see in the design. Copy the dictation on the bottom of the page.

7. Design your own home—Children draw a picture of what they would like their house to look like on the inside.

8. What if—How would you feel?
   Examples: What if you were as tall as your mom?
             How would you feel if you were a chair that nobody wanted to sit in? How would you convince someone to sit on you?

9. Tell the children to draw what the insides of their bodies look like.

10. The children each pick out their favorite color. Then they find pictures in magazines of that color, cut them out, and paste them in the journal.

C. First Through Third Grade Suggestions:

Offer these suggestions to the children—

1. Draw number pictures using scented paints: food coloring, extracts, water brushes, paper.

2. How old would you like to be and why?

3. Using a mathematical theme, make a "feeling" page—sandpaper, cotton, silky materials, glue dripple (color after dry).

4. What food do you dislike the most? If you had to eat it, what other foods would you have with it? Can you tell how much it weighs?

5. Close your eyes. What do you hear? Take a listening walk and record the sounds by drawing a picture of the sound in the journal.

6. Draw a picture of your favorite number.

7. Make up your own mathematics game.

8. Devise a measuring system—define unit and measure five or six things in the room.

9. Design and colonize an island. Tell all about who lives there; how many people, animals, trees, and wild things are on the island?

10. Invent a new toy that teaches adding and subtracting.

11. Find some mathematical problems in a newspaper. Cut out articles and put in the journal.

12. Observe one particular school situation over a period of time. Write about it. How can the school save money?

13. Draw a floor plan for: (a) school, (b) community, (c) city/county, (d) state, (e) country, (f) continent, (g) world.

14. Draw a route you take from home to school. How many blocks and miles is it?

15. Write about "all about me" and how you feel about mathematics.

16. What you would like to be if you were grown up?

17. If you were the principal, what would you do to raise money for the school?

18. Pretend you are an ant in the middle of (park, beach, downtown street). What is your life like? How many people do you see in one day? How many times bigger than you are the people?

19. How would it feel to be a piece of bubble gum in someone's mouth? Write about it. Would you ever change?

20. What's your favorite mathematics lesson? Why do you like it?

21. Write a poem about place value.

22. Crumple foil. What do you see?

23. Design the _____ of the future.

24. If you were writing for a comic section in a newspaper, what would you put in it?

25. In the year 2001, what will your family look like?

26. Write a letter to invite someone to your school (house, city). Tell them all of the things you think they would like, especially about the mathematics class.

27. You are a famous artist. Create a brand new shape that will impress everyone.

28. You are a famous scientist. Create a brand new machine to help people to learn to multiply.

29. You are a new cell in a body. What is your life going to be like?

30. Take an imaginary trip into the inside of your body. What do you find there?

31. Write a new children's story about monsters and fractions.

32. Find symmetry patterns in nature; press between two heavy books. When dry, mount with glue in your journal. Identify plants by measuring them and labeling them.

33. Create two pages of translational symmetry patterns.

34. If you got very fat, how much would you weigh? Draw a picture of yourself.

35. Try to think of the most difficult mathematics test for your teacher to take. Have the teacher take the test. Check the work and give the teacher a grade and a report card.

CONCEPT: Reading the Calendar by Days

TORN PAPER BULLETIN BOARD CALENDAR

Materials: Large bulletin board covered with colored construction paper
Multicolored construction paper
Cotton balls
Scissors
Paste or glue

Procedure:

1. For a selected month (i.e., December) cover a bulletin board with construction paper.

2. Decide on a composition and subject and tear construction paper into shapes to reproduce the idea. Paste the torn pieces onto the bulletin board covered with construction paper.

3. With strips of black construction paper, make a 5-by-7-inch calendar grid. Have the children cut out the numerals for the dates and insert in the proper cell of the grid.

4. Change each month by making new torn paper illustrations.

FANCY SWIRL CALENDARS

Materials: Powdered tempera paint in various colors
Large flat aluminum cake pans (three or four)
White paper, 9-by-12 inches and 12-by-18 inches
Small jars (old baby food jars)
Turpentine, soap, and a stick
Paper towels for cleanup

Procedure:

1. Pour a few ounces of turpentine into a baby food jar and add about a tablespoon of powdered tempera paint to the turpentine. Cover with cap and shake well. Mix about five or six jars of colors (red, yellow, blue, green, black, violet).

2. In each aluminum cake pan, place about 1 inch of water and pour two or three colors from the turpentine mixture over the surface of the water. Turpentine colors will float on the water. Vary color combinations in each pan.

3. Swirl the colors around with a stick. Carefully lay a sheet of white paper over the colored swirled surface. The paper will pick up the pattern.

4. Allow to dry.

5. On a 12-by-18-inch sheet of white paper, mount the swirl design. Make a calendar grid underneath the design. Do one for each month. You may want to ditto a grid for the days and weeks of each month. The children can cut out the grid and add the dates.

 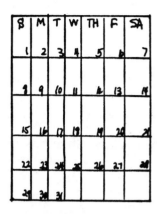

6. Staple across the top or use the Japanese Binding Method described in the Appendix to secure the twelve months together.

CONCEPT: Relating Months to Specific Events

MONTHLY SHADOWBOX SCENES

Materials: Shoe box for each child   Scraps of cloth of various colors
    Construction paper   Scissors
    Glue   Watercolors
    Toothpicks   Brushes
    Cotton   Found natural objects

Procedure:

 1. Assign a month to a child. Have the child use a shoe box to construct a shadowbox scene depicting one important event in that month.

 2. Children can construct houses from construction paper, using natural grasses and plants for trees. Instruct the children to begin by first painting the background before adding characters to the scenes.

YEARLY GRAFFITI

Materials: Mural paper
    Masking tape
    Tempera paint
    Crayons

Procedure:

 1. Cover one whole wall with white mural paper and masking tape. (See "The Art of Graffiti," *School Arts Magazine*, Vol. 72, No. 4, December, 1972, pages 6-8.)

2. Subdivide the wall into twelve sections. Assign two children to a section. Assign one month to each section. Instruct the children assigned to a month and section to find out what is the most important day in that month. Illustrate it in the section using either crayons or tempera. Felt-tip markers often bleed through the paper and soil the walls so it is suggested that you use the materials stated above.

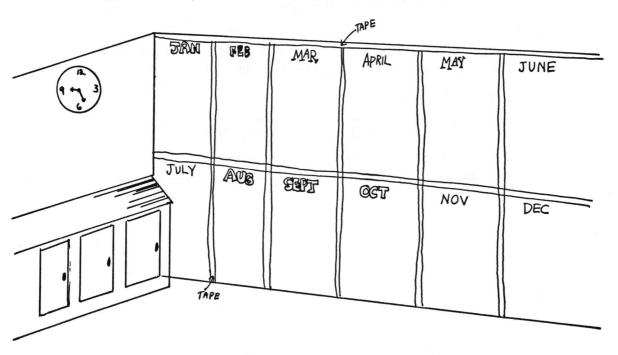

3. If you decide not to cover the wall first, have the children work on the floor on their section and tape the sections up onto the wall one by one. Allow the children to add any idea related to a specific month as they see necessary.

"ALL ABOUT ME" BIOGRAPHY

Materials: Paper   Yarn
             Magic Markers Yarn needle
             Crayons   Paper hole punch

Procedure:

1. Have each child make an "All About Me" autobiographical book. Pages can be illustrated when appropriate. Each activity should be one page.

    Page 1— My Name _____
              Today _____
                     Month   Day   Year

    Page 2— This is what I looked like when I was born.

              I was born _____
                     Month   Day   Year

    Page 3— This is my hand. (Trace hand.)

    Page 4— This is my foot. (Trace foot.) This is my shoe size: _____

    Page 5— This is the first thing I remember. I was about _____ years old when I remember this incident.

    Page 6— This is how I looked when I began school.

              I started school _____
                     Month   Day   Year

Page 7— This is what I do during the fall.

The fall months are _____.
Page 8— This is what I do during the winter.

The winter months are _____.
Page 9— This is what I do during spring.

The spring months are _____.
Page 10—This is what I do during the summer.

The summer months are _____.
Page 11—This is a number line of the years I lived on this earth.

Born	1 yr. old	2 yr. old	
1980	1981	1982	1983

Past   Present   Future

Page 12—This is what I will do in the future when I grow up.
        (Draw a picture of some profession.)

Page 13—This is my height _____.

Page 14—This is my weight _____.

Page 15—This is my telephone number _____.

Page 16—This is my family. I have _____ brothers and _____ sisters.

Page 17—This is my house and address _____.

Page 18—These are my favorite addition problems _____.

Page 19—This is a test I designed for my teacher on ____(date)____.
        (Teacher takes test.)

Page 20—This is the largest number I can write _____.

2. Bind the book using Japanese Binding Method described in the Appendix.

CONCEPT: Telling Time to the Nearest Hour

CRAYON RESISTS AND THE HOURS

Materials: Large clock on bulletin board
White paper
Crayons
Brush
Watercolors
Water jars

Procedure:

1. Make a large clock on a bulletin board.

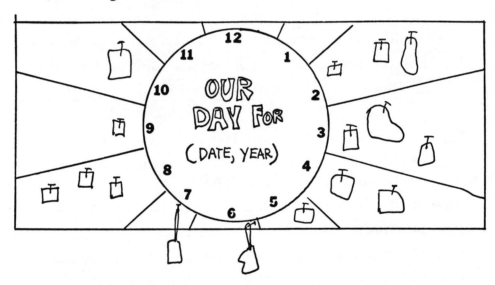

Allow space around the clock to hang children's pictures.

2. Have the children draw what they might be doing at various times during the day. Assign specific morning activities to one group of children, afternoon activities to another group, and evening activities to a third group. After children color illustrations of activities, have them paint over the crayon drawings with watercolors. The paint will be absorbed by the uncolored parts of the paper.

3. Have the children insert the drawings in the proper hour sections.

PAPER PLATE CLOCKS

Materials: Paper plates
Crayons
Two clock hands (one large, one small)
Brass fastener

Procedure:

1. The children make clocks from the paper plates.

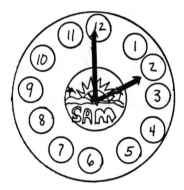

2. They decorate the center with crayon and insert hands with fastener. Each child puts his or her name on clock.

3. Call out special times and have the children place the hands on the hours.
   —At what time do you get up?
   —At what time do you start school?
   —At what time do you eat lunch?
   —At what time do you go for physical education?

4. Have the children hang their clocks in an appropriate place in the classroom and arrange the hands when they are "IN" the room and when they are "OUT" of the room.

5. A worksheet is provided on page 234 for your convenience if you choose to expand on procedure 3 and have the children draw in the hands.

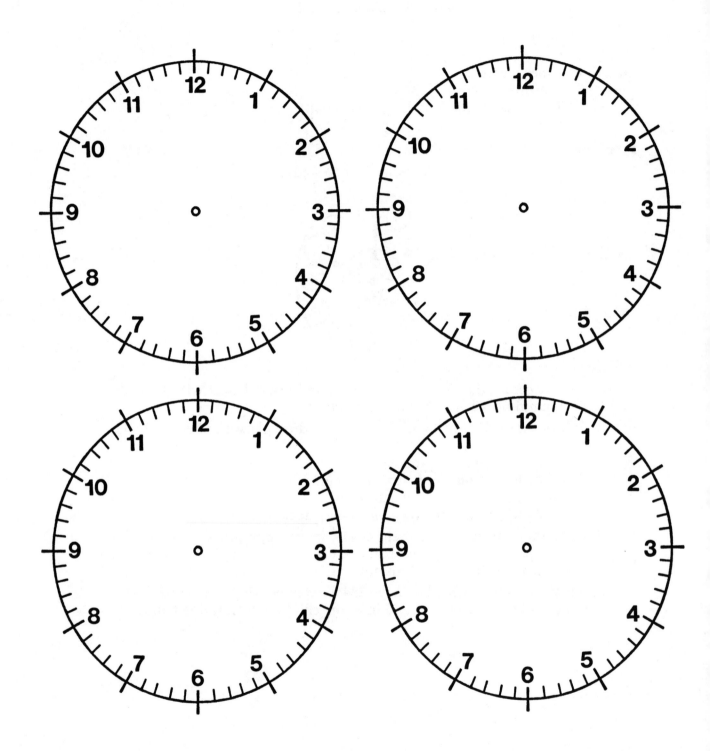

234

Section 12

CREATIVE PROBLEM-SOLVING IDEAS

To the teacher

This last section presents a multitude of creative problem-solving situations for the primary child and is divided into three parts.

The first part presents a review and introduction to specific problem-solving skills. It is subdivided into school months. You may want to coordinate the problems to the school year or select problems that can be adapted to any time of the year. Personalize these problem-solving situations by using the students and the classroom for fact finding and data collecting. Specific problem-solving skills included in this section are fact finding, true/false statements, addition, subtraction, multiplication and division situations, estimating, classification problems, and graphing, including coordinate geometry.

The second part presents a series of ideas you may want to reproduce on a ditto for your classes. These ideas are creative, inventive, and unique. They are designed to provide some fun in the mathematics class after the paper-and-pencil tasks are completed. Enjoy this section and its suggestions.

The last part of Section 12 provides daily activities for the children for a Summer Mathematics Homework Calendar. These can be reproduced and sent home at the end of the school year with the child. You may want to adapt the calendar to the special needs of individual children or the entire class. The calendar is designed for a K-3 grade level.

CONCEPT: Solving Problems—September Through May

Materials: Teacher-made worksheets from suggested activities

Procedure: Read the section. Choose appropriate problem-solving skill for children. Rewrite to meet your students' needs.

MONTH: September   THEME: School—Getting to Know Your New Friends

---

FACTS ABOUT YOUR CLASS

a. Who is the tallest _____ shortest _____?

b. Who has the longest/shortest hair? _____.

c. How many children have brown, black, blond, or red hair? _____

d. How many in the class are boys _____ girls _____ squirrels _____?

e. How many in the class wear glasses _____ ?
   do not wear glasses _____?

f. How many own a pet _____?

g. How many ride the bus _____ walk _____ to school?

h. Who lived in a state other than the one the child is presently living?
   Name _____
   State _____
   Foreign country _____

i. Who speaks a language other than English?
   Name _____
   Language _____

You may wish to add more to the list. When the children have completed their fact finding, have each child draw a self-portrait and place the following facts on the portrait. Place the portraits on the bulletin board or make a class portrait book.

FACTS ABOUT MYSELF

Name _____   Birthday _____

Nickname _____   Age _____

Color eyes _____   Hair _____

Height _____   Sex _____

Weight _____

Likes _____

Dislikes _____

TRUE/FALSE STATEMENTS ABOUT THE CLASS

Take the facts collected from activity No. 1 and the self-portrait facts book and make up a True/False statement worksheet about the class.

Circle One

1. Mary Hayes is the tallest in the class.	True False
2. Brett Taylor is the teacher.	True False
3. Rebecca McIntyre wears glasses.	True False
4. Christy Rogers speaks Spanish.	True False
5. Mrs. Stella Barry teaches second grade.	True False
6. Shem Lewis was born on January 4, 1978.	True False
7. Rangel Dockery likes peanut butter.	True False
8. Anna Conomos dislikes cookies.	True False
9. Susan Koehler's nickname is Suzie.	True False
10. Debbie Levine is 5'9" tall.	True False

Suggestion to the teacher: Make up a scavenger hunt. Type worksheet as suggested above but delete the name. Have the children search for the person that fits the fact.

1. _____ is the tallest in class.	True False
2. _____ is the teacher.	True False

ASKING THE RIGHT QUESTION

This is a game, based upon the facts collected in the class, which you can play with the class. Ask the following questions of the class and have the children figure out the correct answer. This game can be played individually or in small groups. The groups may be competitive.

1. What is the difference in inches between the tallest child in class and shortest?

2. Who wears more sneakers—boys or girls?

3. Who has more dogs as pets—boys or girls?

4. Who has more cats as pets—boys or girls?

5. How many books are in the classroom? _____ True   False

6. How many hours are spent in the classroom during a school day?
   Hours _____ Minutes _____

7. List two facts about the teacher:
   Fact one _____
   Fact two _____
   Ask the teacher a question about the two facts gathered that will provide more information about the teacher.

8. Who wears more blue jeans—boys or girls?

9. Where is the principal?

10. Who knows the name of the principal? building engineer? librarian? secretary?

MONTH: October   THEME: Halloween/Adding Problems

PUTTING THINGS TOGETHER

1. Karen has 9 fish. Mary has 3 fish. How many fish will there be if they are placed in one bowl? _9 + 3 = 12_

2. Look at your friend's shoes. Count the number of holes in each shoe where you place the shoelace through. How many holes are there all together?

3. Count your shoelace holes. How many do you have? How many do you have with yours and your friend's?

4. What is the largest page number in your reading book? What is the largest page number in your math book? How many pages are there all together?

5. How many thumbs are there all together when you and your friend are playing?

6. Count your friend's crayons. Count your crayons. How many are there all together? How many crayons do you and your friend have that are:

	Friend		Mine		
blue?	_____	+	_____	=	_____
red?	_____	+	_____	=	_____
green?	_____	+	_____	=	_____
yellow?	_____	+	_____	=	_____
brown?	_____	+	_____	=	_____
magenta?	_____	+	_____	=	_____
white?	_____	+	_____	=	_____
ecru?	_____	+	_____	=	_____

7. You and your friend are to draw a Halloween pumpkin with a face. How many teeth does your pumpkin have? How many teeth are there all together in both yours and your friend's drawing? Write the number sentence.

8. Make a drawing of a witch's cookie. Put some raisins, chocolate chips, and nuts in the cookie. Write a number sentence that shows the total of the many different things you put in the cookie.

9. A witch had 8 toes on one foot and 5 toes on the other. How many toes are there? Make a drawing of the witch and write out the number sentence. __8 + 5 = 13_____

10. A goblin had 2 eyes, 1 nose, and 32 fingers. Make a drawing of the goblin. Make a number sentence that shows the number of fingers on each hand that makes a total of 32 fingers.

11. Peppino attends a galaxy school called Way Out Elementary. He needs Space Star Kick shoes for physical education. Last year his Space Star Kick shoes were 9 inches long. This year he needed to purchase 10-inch shoes. When he hung them toe to toe from his travel desk, they were dangling behind him. How long was the string of shoes? Draw a picture of Peppino's travel desk and dangling shoes.

12. Brunhilda the witch met Spooky the ghost on Halloween night. They decided to have a late dinner. Brunhilda mixed the following recipe: 1 pinch of critter dust, 118 milliliters of warm pumpkin milk. She shook it well and gave it to Spooky. Then she made him a muck cookie from 117 milliliters of prepackaged cookie muck. How many milliliters of food did Spooky eat in all? __118 + 117 = 235_____

MONTH: November   THEME: Thanksgiving/Subtracting/Adding

TAKING THINGS AWAY/PUTTING THINGS TOGETHER

1. A pilgrim had 14 ears of corn. The turkeys ate 5 ears of corn. How many ears were left? ___14 - 5 = 9___

2. Doreen baked 129 pies. Of these pies, 82 were pumpkin. How many were not pumpkin pies? Write the number sentence. 129 - 82 = 47

3. Mother Goose made 200 million pounds of dressing. Ducky Lucky ate 100 million pounds of it. How much dressing was left? Draw a picture or write a story about Mother Goose and Ducky Lucky's dressing.

$$
\begin{array}{r}
200,000,000 \\
-\ 100,000,000 \\
\hline
100,000,000
\end{array}
$$

4. A turkey had 25,673 feathers. Of these feathers, 14,680 were light grey and 3,891 were black. The rest of the feathers were white. How many white feathers did the turkey have? a. 14,680 + 3,891 = 18,571

   b. 25,673 - 18,571 = 7,102

5. There were 35 cranberries in a bowl. Jim-Jim squashed 10 cranberries between his fingers. Jody smashed 4 cranberries between her fingers. How many cranberries were not in the mess? Draw a picture of the mess.
   a. ___10 + 4 = 14___   b. ___35 - 14 = 21___

6. A squirrel rolled 14 walnuts into his nest. Then he rolled 29 walnuts into his nest. Over the weekend he ate 5 walnuts. How many walnuts were left in his nest? Draw the picture and write out the number sentences to solve the problem. a. 14 + 29 = 43 b. 43 - 5 = 38

Super Problem:

7. There were 124 pilgrims and 41 Indians who sat down at the Thanksgiving dinner. On the table there were 14 turkeys, 9 dishes of corn on the cob, 15 bowls of sweet potatoes, 6 molds of lime jello, 8 bowls of mixed green vegetables, 15 loaves of bread, 12 bowls of cranberry sauce, 60 apples, and 25 large pumpkin pies with whipping cream. Write the number sentences for each of the following problems.

   a. How many plates did they have to set at the table for each of the dinner guests? __124 + 41 = 165 Pilgrims and Indians__
   b. The men ate 8 turkeys. How many were left for the ladies who ate the rest? __14 - 8 = 6 Turkeys__

c. The Indians ate 4 dishes of corn. The pilgrims ate 4 dishes of corn. How many dishes did they eat all together? **4+4=8 Dishes of corn**

d. The young boys ate 2 bowls of sweet potatoes and the young girls ate 3 bowls of sweet potatoes. How much were left for the adults who ate the rest? **2+3=5; 15-5=10 sweet Potatoes**

e. Everyone loved the lime jello molds. No jello mold was left after the dinner. How much was eaten? **6-6=0 lime Jellos**

f. The pilgrims passed 5 bowls of mixed green vegetables to the Indians. The Indians passed 3 bowls to the pilgrims. How many bowls of mixed green vegetables were passed around? Only 4 bowls were eaten up. **5+3=8 Mixed green vegetables**

g. The pilgrims and Indians broke the bread together and gave a special thanksgiving to God for the good year. They all ate 1 piece of bread. Each loaf was cut into exactly 11 pieces. How many pieces of bread were left over after eating 1 piece each? **15×11 = 165** **165 - 165 = 0 Loaves**

h. The guests over 50 years old ate 4 bowls of cranberry sauce. The guests under 15 years old ate 2 bowls of cranberry sauce. How many bowls were left for those who were between the ages of 15 and 50 who ate the rest? **4+2=6; 12-6=6 Cranberry sauce**

i. Each guest wanted an apple. How many more apples were needed to provide each guest with an apple? **165-60=105 apples needed**

j. For dessert the young boys ate 7 pumpkin pies, the young girls ate 6 pumpkin pies, and the adults ate 10 pumpkin pies. How many pies were left? **7+6+10=23; 25-23=2 pumpkin pies**

k. Can you figure out how much food was eaten and left over when the meal was finished? This is tricky to figure out. Read the problems well and make sure you have the right answers.

Turkeys **0**
Corn on the cob **1**
Sweet potatoes **0**
Lime jello **0**
Mixed green vegetables **4**
Loaves of bread **0**
Cranberry sauce **0**
Apples **0**
Pumpkin pies **2**

Note to Teacher: Instruct the children to make a class wall mural of this Thanksgiving dinner with the pilgrims and Indians. If the food is made out of construction paper and taped to the table, the children can visually work out the problems by untaping and retaping the food to the table.

MONTH: December   THEME: Winter/Number Patterns, Adding, Subtracting, Multiplication

---

FINDING A PATTERN

1. On the chalkboard write the following patterns and have the children predict the next item by coloring each pattern on a grid sheet and filling in the proper color to complete the pattern.

a. Red, Red, Yellow, Red, _Red_ .

b. Blue, Yellow, Green, Red, Blue, Yellow, _Green_ , Red.

c. Brown, Black, White, White, Black, _Brown_ .

d. Orange, Black, Orange, Black, Orange, _Black_ .

e. Yellow, Orange, Black, Orange, Yellow, Yellow, Orange, _Black_ , Orange, _Yellow_ .

f. Red, Red, Black, Red, Red, Yellow, Red, Red, Black, Red, Red, _Yellow_ , _Red_ , _Red_ , _Black_ .

g. Red, Yellow, Blue, Red, Yellow, _Blue_ , _Red_ , _Yellow_ , Blue.

h. Green, Red, Yellow, Yellow, Red, _Green_ , _Green_ , Red, Yellow, _Yellow_ , _Red_ , _Green_ .

i. Blue, White, Red, Red, Red, _Blue_ , _white_ , Red, Red, Red.

j. Black, White, Black, White, _Black_ , _white_ , _Black_ , _White_ .

2. Number patterns:
a. 2, 4, 6, 8, _10_, _12_, 14, _16_.
b. 4, 8, 12, 16, _20_, 24, _28_, _32_.
c. 2, 3, 4, 5, _6_, _7_, 8, _9_, _10_, _11_, 12.
d. 1, 3, 5, 7, _9_, 11, 13, 15, _17_, _19_.
e. 0, 0, 1, 0, 0, 1, 0, 0, _1_, _0_, _0_, 1.
f. 1, 1, 1, 1, 5, 1, 1, 1, 1, 5, _1_, _1_, 1, 1, _5_.
g. 0, 5, 10, 15, _20_, 25, 30, _35_, _40_, 45, _50_.
h. 98, 97, 96, 95, 94, _93_, _92_, 91, _90_, 89, 88, _87_.
i. 30, 27, 24, 21, 18, _15_, _12_, 9, _6_, 3.
j. 100, 0, 99, 1, 98, 2, 97, 3, 96, _4_, 95, _5_, _94_, 6, _93_, _7_.
k. 1, 2, 3, 5, 8, 13, _21_, _34_, 55.
l. 1, 2, 3, 8, 16, _32_, _64_, 128.
m. 100; 1,000; 10,000; _100,000_; _1,000,000_; 10,000,000.
n. 249, 251, 253, 255, _257_, _259_, 261.

ADDING/SUBTRACTING/MULTIPLYING PROBLEMS

SANTA'S TOY HOUSE: For the holidays, Santa's Toy Elves made the following toys in one day:

    14 Dolls
     2 Electric Trains
    10 Teddy Bears
     3 Video Games
     5 Dartboard Games
     7 Watercolor Sets
     9 Sets of Building Blocks
     8 Doll Houses
     1 Box of Fudge

1. Betty Lynch had 3 girlfriends and 2 boyfriends. She wanted to give each friend a gift for the holidays. How many gifts must she buy for her friends? _3 + 2 = 5_

2. If Betty buys 2 dolls, 1 electric train, and 3 teddy bears, how many toys would be left at Santa's shop after one day's work? How many extra presents would she have? What are they? _2 + 1 + 3 = 6_ ;
_14 + 2 + 10 + 3 + 5 + 7 + 9 + 8 + 1 = 59_ ;
59 − 6 = 53 TOYS LEFT.

3 M. Bridges was a Boy Scout Leader. He decided to buy video games for all the boys in his scout troup. He figured it would take 9 days for the elves to make enough video games for the boys in his scout troup. How many boys are in his scout troup? _3×9 = 27 Boys in Scout Troop._

4. The elves worked 20 days in November. How many electric trains did they make in November? _20×2 = 40 Electric Trains._

5. In December the elves worked 24 days. How many teddy bears and doll houses did they make in December? _24×10 = 240 teddy_, _24×8 = 192 doll_
240 + 192 = 432 total.   bears   houses

6. In the total year, the elves worked 205 days. How many boxes of fudge did they make? _205 × 1 = 205 boxes of fudge._

7. Mary Ann knew 14 girls and 7 boys. She wanted to buy them all watercolor sets for the holidays. How many days would it take the elves to make enough watercolor sets for Mary Ann? _14×7 = 21, 21÷7 = 3._

8. How many different toys did the elves make in one day? _59 toys._

Super Problem:

9. How many toys did the elves make in one year? They worked every day except Sunday. _1983: 365−52 = 313_ , _313 × 59 = 18,467 toys_
_1984: 365 − 53 = 312_ , _312 × 59 = 18,408 toys._

MONTH: January   **THEME: Time, Days, Months/Multiplying, Dividing**

TIME, MONTHS, DAYS PROBLEMS

1. Cheryl's toes were cold on Monday from 3:10 P.M. to 7:30 P.M. On Tuesday they were cold from 4:35 P.M. to 6:15 P.M. On Wednesday they were cold from 8:00 A.M. to 9:00 A.M. Then she put on a double pair of socks. How many hours and minutes were Cheryl's toes cold all together? Why were Cheryl's toes cold at those times? Write a story about it. _____

_____ , _____ , _____

2. Marian made some resolutions for the New Year. She said, "I will not eat candy bars on Sunday, Tuesday, or Thursday for the rest of the year." What are the total number of days in the rest of the year she will eat a candy bar? _____ , _____ , _____ , _____ .

3. Walter rides his bicycle to school every school day. He rides a total of 40 miles a week. How many miles does he ride in 1 day of a 5-day school week? _____

4. Jean walks to school on Monday, Tuesday, and Thursday. She walks a total of 15 miles each week. How many miles does she walk in one day?

5. Carmela goes to work on Monday, Tuesday, Wednesday, and Thursday. She works 32 hours a week. How many hours does she work in one day?

_____

6. A building has a family of nine mice living in it. In January, February, and March they live on the first floor. In April, May, and June they live on the second floor. During July, August, and September they live at the beach and they return to the first floor during October, November, and December. How many months do they live on the first floor? How many days do they spend at the beach? How many weeks do they live on the second floor? Write a story about the mice family from the facts presented here.

_____, _____, _____, _____, _____

SEARCHING FOR ANSWERS: LISTENING AND THINKING

You can present the following think problems. Have the children write the answers on a piece of paper.

1. Think of an even number between 22 and 26: ___24___
2. Think of an odd number between 9 and 13: ___11___
3. Think of two even numbers that are less than 10 and will add up to 14: ___6 + 8___
4. Can you find two odd numbers less than 13 that add up to 20? ___9 + 11___
5. Can you find 3 numbers in sequence under 6 that add up to 6? ___1 + 2 + 3___
6. What number under 10 is missing from this sequence? 3, 5, 9, 2, 8, 4, 7, 6 ___1___
7. What is the largest number you can write that is less than 19,972 and more than 2? ___19,971___
8. What is the second to the last number in the sequence? 3, 4, 9, 8, 5, 1, 6, 0 ___6___
9. What is the fourth number in the sequence? 13, 41, 82, 19, 31, 552, 66 ___19___
10. If you add 2 ten times and 3 ten times what is your answer? ___50___

MONTH: February   THEME: Estimating

ESTIMATING LARGE NUMBERS

Estimate the following and write the answers on a sheet of paper.

1. Estimate the number of children in the classroom. Can you estimate how many children are in the school? (Hint: Count the number of classrooms and multiply that number by the number of children in your classroom.)

2. Estimate the number of pencils in the school if each child has an average of two pencils.

3. Estimate the number of ditto worksheets you do in one week. Can you figure out how many your class needs in one day?

4. Estimate the number of cans in your family's cupboard. (Hint: Count a sample on a shelf and then the number on the shelves.)

MONTH: March   THEME: Classification Skills, Addition

SPRING ATTRIBUTE BOOKS

1. Make up a ditto master sheet with a large egg shape on it. Then tell the children the following situation. A rabbit delivers some interesting Spring Holiday eggs problem sheets. In fact, they are very special egg-problem worksheets. The children are to find pictures stated on the worksheet. Each child should have five worksheets over a period of a week and fill in the egg with pictures found in magazines.

2. Cut and paste the picture with the appropriate attribute in the egg region. The five worksheets could be labeled with the following attributes: round things, square things, big things, small things. When finished cutting and pasting the first four worksheets, have the children count the number of pictures in each egg and write the total in the right-hand corner. Then ask the children to add up all of the items and write the grand total on the worksheet that is the Special Number egg (5 + 7 + 4 + 9 = 25).

3. You can now make up the following word problems based on the children's own work:

    a. Mary has 7 round things in her picture. John has 3. How many round things are there all together?

    b. Roberto has _____ square things and Rita has _____. How many are there all together?

    c. Or you may make the following Scavenger Hunt Worksheet on Attribute Problems.

ATTRIBUTE BOOK PROBLEMS

Write the name of a friend in the blank and the number from a page in the book in the second blank. Work out the number sentences.

_____ has _____ round things
_____ has _____ round things
_____ + _____ = _____ round things

_____ has _____ square things
_____ has _____ square things
_____ + _____ = _____ square things

_____ has _____ big things
_____ has _____ big things
_____ + _____ = _____ big things

_____ has _____ small things
_____ has _____ small things
_____ + _____ = _____ small things

_____ has a total of _____ objects
_____ has a total of _____ objects
_____ + _____ = _____ objects

Trick questions:
_____ has a total of _____ objects
_____ has _____ round things
_____ – _____ round things = _____ objects

_____ has a total of _____ objects
_____ has _____ small things
_____ has _____ big things
_____ objects + _____ small things – _____ big things = _____ objects

This sample worksheet may be elaborated upon by you depending on the specific needs of your class. The problems can be converted to multiplication and division problems. Other Special Attribute egg worksheets might include:

Shapes (squares, circles, triangles)
Colors (unlimited)
Hard/soft objects
Long/short objects
Animals (farm, jungle, city)
Plants (flowers, trees, leaves, weeds, vegetables)

Nonliving things
People: (elderly, young, parents, children, teenagers)
Transportation: (cars, trains, planes, etc.)

MONTH: April   THEME: Multiplication, Table Making/Graphing

MAKING A TABLE AND GRAPHING

1. An ice cream cone costs 15¢. Show through a table how much 10 ice cream cones will cost.

Number of cones	1	2	3	4	5	6	7	8	9	10
Total cost	15	30								

2. A spider has 8 legs. Show through a table how many spider legs there are when there is more than one spider.

Number of spiders	1	2	3	4	5	6	7	8	9	10
Number of legs	8	16								

3. A big truck has 6 wheels on it. Show through a table how many wheels there are with 5, 8, 10, and 12 trucks.

Number of trucks	1	2	3	4	5	6	7	8	9	10	11	12
Number of wheels	6	12										

4. A picture graph is a graph that shows through pictures a representation of a number. Make a picture graph that shows the number of books in your classroom. The teacher needs to make up the following worksheet.
   Room _____ Textbooks and Magazines
   ☐ = 2 Books or Magazines

Math Books	☐ ☐ ☐ ☐ ☐ ☐ ☐ ☐ ☐ ☐ ☐
Language Arts	☐ ☐ ☐ ☐ ☐ ☐ ☐ ☐
Spelling	☐ ☐ ☐ ☐ ☐ ☐ ☐ ☐ ☐
Basal Readers	☐ ☐ ☐ ☐ ☐ ☐ ☐ ☐ ☐
Magazines	☐ ☐ ☐ ☐ ☐ ☐
Science	☐ ☐ ☐ ☐ ☐ ☐ ☐ ☐ ☐ ☐

5. A bar graph is a picture. A bar graph shows through bars of color a representation of a number. Make a bar graph that shows the number of times each letter of the alphabet appears on a sample paragraph from your Basal Reader. See the sample grid on page 249.

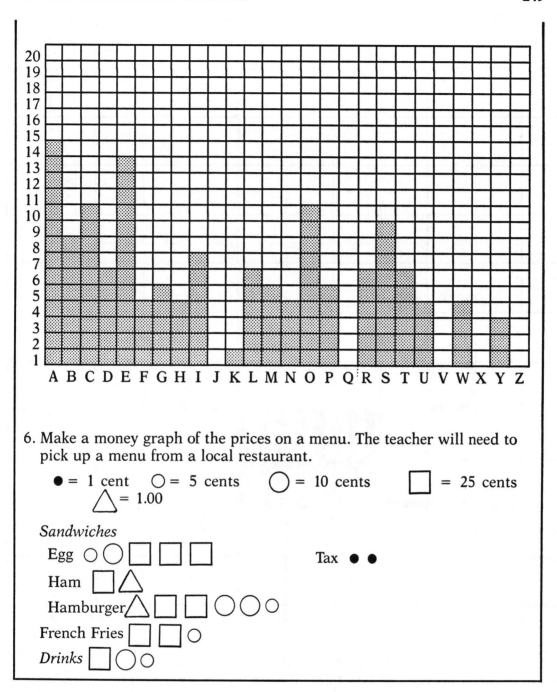

6. Make a money graph of the prices on a menu. The teacher will need to pick up a menu from a local restaurant.

● = 1 cent   ◌ = 5 cents   ◯ = 10 cents   ☐ = 25 cents
△ = 1.00

Sandwiches

Egg ◌ ◌ ☐ ☐ ☐   Tax ● ●

Ham ☐ △

Hamburger △ ☐ ☐ ◯ ◯ ◌

French Fries ☐ ☐ ◌

Drinks ☐ ◯ ◌

MONTH: May   THEME: Coordinate Geometry
Reproduce the worksheets on pages 250-252 and follow instructions.

DIRECTIONS: Locate each ordered pair on the grid.* Label each point with a letter. Connect the points as you go along.

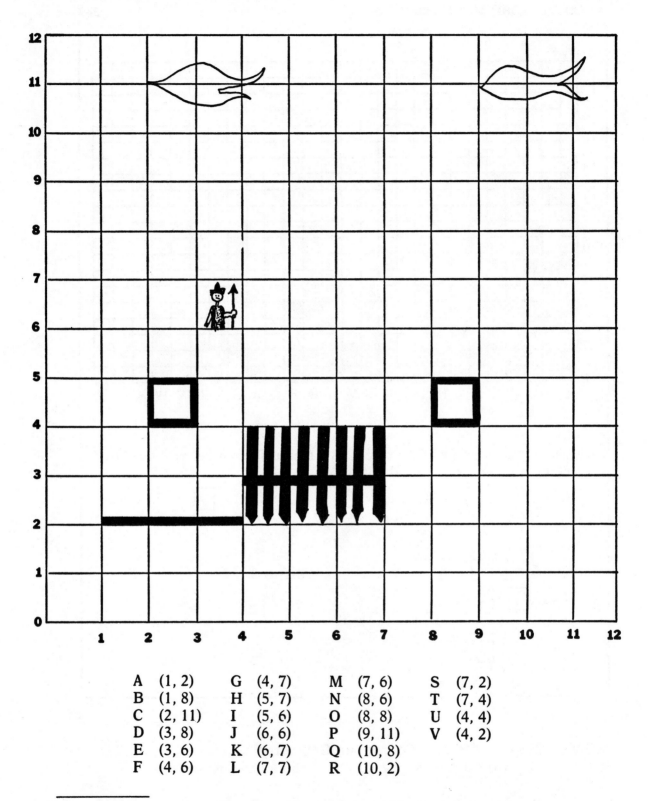

A	(1, 2)	G	(4, 7)	M	(7, 6)	S	(7, 2)
B	(1, 8)	H	(5, 7)	N	(8, 6)	T	(7, 4)
C	(2, 11)	I	(5, 6)	O	(8, 8)	U	(4, 4)
D	(3, 8)	J	(6, 6)	P	(9, 11)	V	(4, 2)
E	(3, 6)	K	(6, 7)	Q	(10, 8)		
F	(4, 6)	L	(7, 7)	R	(10, 2)		

*This material is reprinted by permission from Unit 25, *Multiplication and Motion*, Minnesota Mathematics and Science Teaching Project (MINNEMAST), a grant from the National Science Foundation, University of Minnesota, 1970.

DIRECTIONS: Write the ordered pair in the grid space below.* Connect the points as you go along.

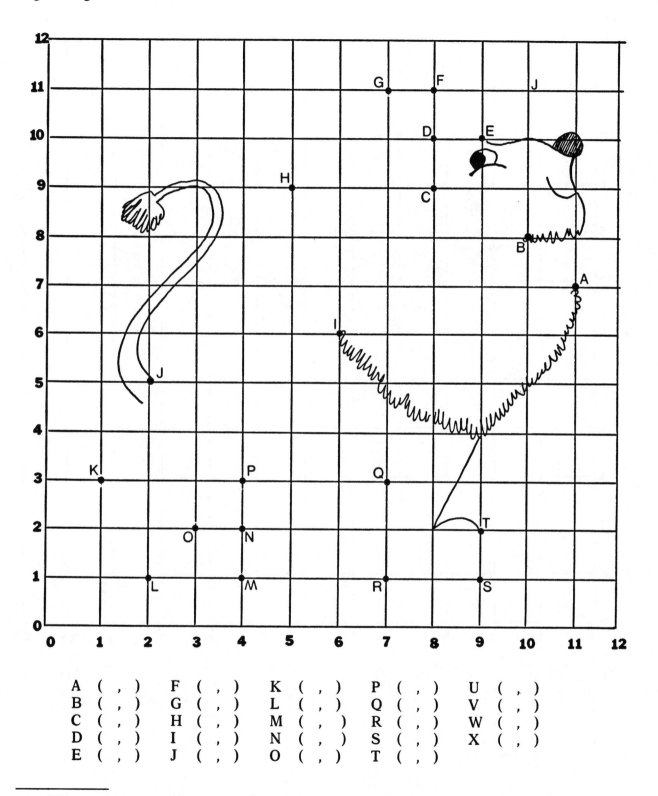

A (,) F (,) K (,) P (,) U (,)
B (,) G (,) L (,) Q (,) V (,)
C (,) H (,) M (,) R (,) W (,)
D (,) I (,) N (,) S (,) X (,)
E (,) J (,) O (,) T (,)

*This material is reprinted by permission from Unit 25, (CFAS2Multiplication and Motion, Minnesota Mathematics and Science Teaching Project (MINNEMAST), a grant from the National Science Foundation, University of Minnesota, 1970.

DIRECTIONS: Write the ordered pairs in the space below. Connect the points as you go along.

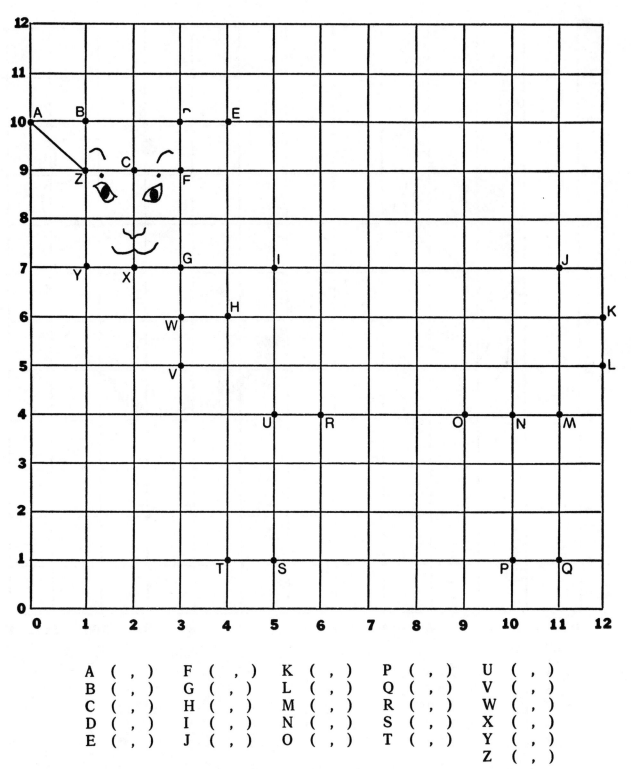

A (,) F (,) K (,) P (,) U (,)
B (,) G (,) L (,) Q (,) V (,)
C (,) H (,) M (,) R (,) W (,)
D (,) I (,) N (,) S (,) X (,)
E (,) J (,) O (,) T (,) Y (,)
                                    Z (,)

© 1984 by Prentice-Hall, Inc.

*This material is reprinted by permission from Unit 25, *Multiplication and Motion*, Minnesota Mathematics and Science Teaching Project (MINNEMAST), a grant from the National Science Foundation, University of Minnesota, 1970.

CONCEPT: Solving Situation Problems

CREATIVE COLORING MATH DITTOS

Materials: Teacher-made ditto worksheets based on suggestions listed here

Procedure:

Select some of the creative coloring ideas from this activity, reproduce on a ditto, and have the children visually solve the problems.

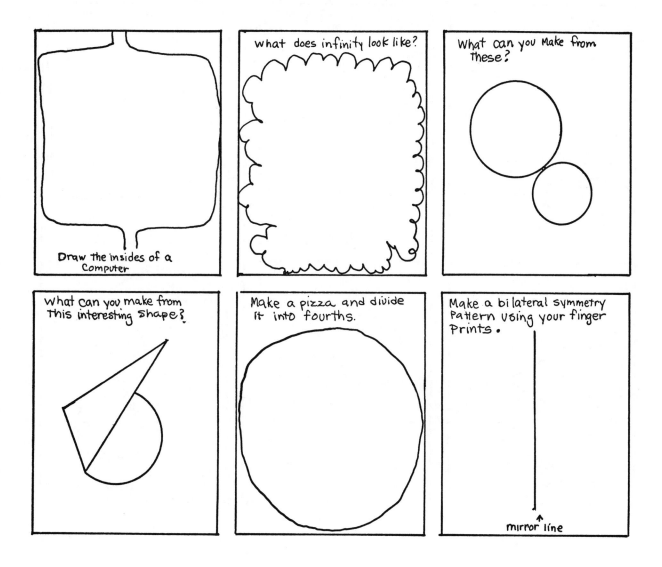

Draw the insides of a Computer

what does infinity look like?

What can you make from these?

what can you make from this interesting shape?

Make a pizza and divide it into fourths.

Make a bilateral symmetry pattern using your finger prints.

mirror line

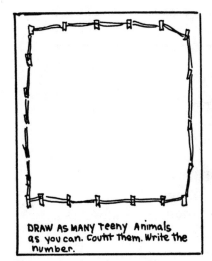

DRAW AS MANY teeny Animals as you can. Count them. Write the number.

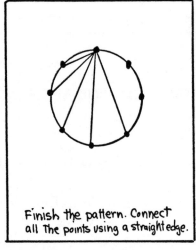

Finish the pattern. Connect all The points using a straight edge.

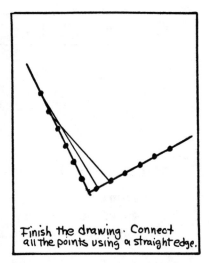

Finish the drawing. Connect all The points using a straight edge.

What do you suppose numbers look like on MARS? Draw them. Draw a Martian Math Teacher.

Paste as many circle things You can find on This page. Look for pictures in magazines.

Paste as many green things You can find on this page.

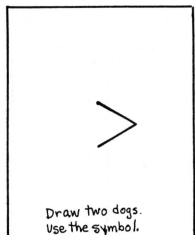

Draw two dogs. Use the symbol.

Draw two snakes. Use the Symbol.

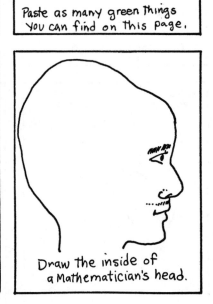

Draw the inside of a Mathematician's head.

Make a symmetrical
Pattern using only squares.

Make a design using
numbers only.

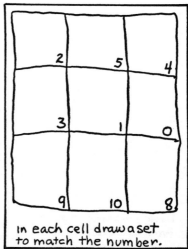

In each cell draw a set
to match the number.

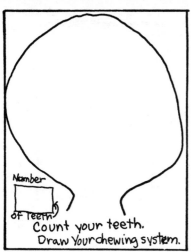

Count your teeth.
Draw your chewing system.

TEACHER

Draw a picture of your teacher.
Label the height, weight and
shoe size of your teacher.

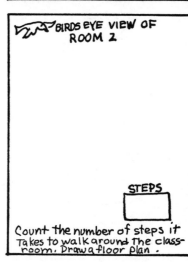

BIRDS EYE VIEW OF
ROOM 2

STEPS

Count the number of steps it
takes to walk around the classroom. Draw a floor plan.

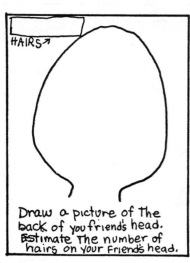

HAIRS

Draw a picture of the
back of you friend's head.
Estimate the number of
hairs on your friend's head.

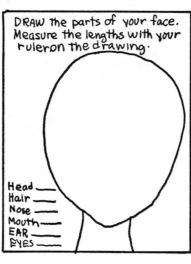

DRAW the parts of your face.
Measure the lengths with your
ruler on the drawing.

Head ___
Hair ___
Nose ___
Mouth ___
EAR ___
EYES ___

DRAW A MAZE between the
Duck and the chicken.

IT FLEW

Design a paper airplane
from this sheet. Fly it.
Measure how far it flew.

1st Prize

Make a line pattern without
lifting your crayon from the
paper.

Cut along the dotted line. Make a
Pin wheel by folding one point
into the middle and securing with
a brass fastener. Rotational sym.

FARM

Draw a farm yard. Put in
1 horse   4 ducks   7 flies
2 cows   5 chicks   8 Ants
3 chickens   6 birds   9 spiders

On The elephant
Draw as many peanuts as you
can. Count them.

Design a Cover for your
Math book.

Population

Draw the inside of an ant hill.
Estimate the population.

Think of the most difficult
Division problem you can.
Put it on this page. Give it to
your Teacher to solve. Check
your Teacher's work.

BRAINBUSTER

Fill the fish bowl with Guppies.
Count Them.

Think of the most difficult 3 digit number to multiply. Give it to your teacher to solve. Check the work.

BRAINBUSTER

GRADE

Punch holes in this paper with a sharp pencil. Count the holes.

THE Holey Paper

← PUNCH HERE

And here

And here

BLUE RIBBON WINNER

Draw a picture of your pet. Measure its height with a ruler.

DRAW IN HERE

Draw a picture of the Teeniest thing you can think of.

Draw a picture of the longest and shortest thing you can think of.

Make up a set of addition and subtraction problems for your parents to solve. Check their work.

1.   2.   3.

4.   5.   6.

7.   8.   GRADE
            W W

Make up a set of Money Problems for your parents to solve. Check their work.

Find the name of a famous Mathematician. Draw a picture of him/her.

FAMOUS MATHEMATICIAN

Make up your own worksheet. Check it. Grade it. Turn it in.

CONCEPT: Retaining Mathematics Skills During Summer Vacation

SUMMER MATHEMATICS HOMEWORK CALENDAR

Materials: Calendars

Procedure:

Reproduce the calendars shown on pages 259-261 and send a copy home with each child on the last day of school. (NOTE: You will have to adapt each calendar to the current year.) Every calendar should be accompanied with your letter to the parent explaining the activities. Instruct the parent to have the child perform the activity suggested for the day in order to help the child retain the skills and concepts acquired over the past year. You may wish to adapt this idea to the special needs of the class and design specific activities.

JUNE

SUNDAY	MONDAY	TUESDAY	WEDNESDAY	THURSDAY	FRIDAY	SATURDAY
					School is out. TAKE A REST.	Think about your best day in school. Tell your parent about it.
Sing a song you learned in school for your Parent.	Count to 50 by 2's if you can, or by 1's if you can.	Name 10 colors and an object that color.	Jump on your right foot 10 times. Jump on your left foot 8 times. Pat your head and belly together—10 X	Walk 100 paces in your yard. Draw a map showing the route you took. Where did you end up?	Tell your parent your name, address, phone number, parent work number and who to contact in case of an emergency.	CLEAN YOUR ROOM. Classify and order your things. Make labels. SHIRTS
Give someone special a gift, but don't tell anyone it was you.	Make a list from A to Z of the furniture in your house. A = Ashtray B = Bed	How high can you count? By 2's By 3's By 4's By 5's	Design a huge adding problem for your parent. Give them the test. Check their work. Grade it.	Subtract your telephone number from your friend's. What is the answer? 431-6200 -298-1341 133-4859	Draw 10 circles. What can you make from each circle.	Fix a Toy That is broken.
Write a Love letter to your Parents.	Count all the fingers and toes in your family. How Many are there? Write Answer here →	Measure your height. Write it down. Weigh yourself. Save it. You will need these records in August.	Draw a picture of yourself. Put on the information ↓ Name Address Height Weight Date	Count the number of foot steps from your front door to the street, around your house and back to your front door.	On the Want Ad section of the newspaper write the numbers and alphabet with a black crayon. 0 to 50	Clean the messiest room in the house Today. Record how long it took you. To clean.
THINK about what you want to be when you grow up.	Make a list of things to do this summer that will involve making a decision.	Grab a handful of Breakfast Cereal. Count the pieces in your hand. Can you estimate how many pieces are in the box?	Make a design that shows rotational or turning symmetry.	Count the number of Jones in the Telephone book. Subtract that number from the largest page number.	Add up all the minutes you watched T.V. today.	Do some yard work for your parent. Charge them 1¢ per minute. Check Time-in and Time-out with your parent.

259

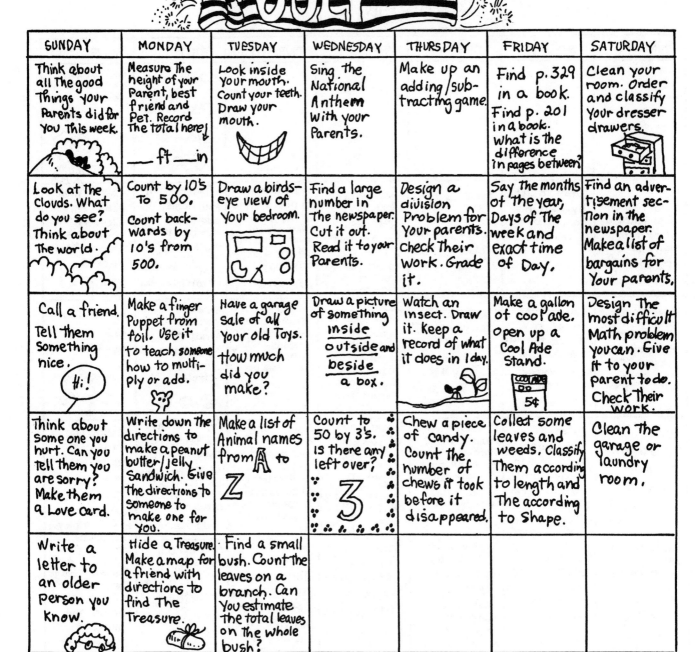

JULY

SUNDAY	MONDAY	TUESDAY	WEDNESDAY	THURSDAY	FRIDAY	SATURDAY
Think about all the good things your parents did for you this week.	Measure the height of your parent, best friend and pet. Record the total here! ___ ft ___ in	Look inside your mouth. Count your teeth. Draw your mouth.	Sing the National Anthem with your parents.	Make up an adding/subtracting game.	Find p.329 in a book. Find p.201 in a book. What is the difference in pages between?	Clean your room. Order and classify your dresser drawers.
Look at the clouds. What do you see? Think about the world.	Count by 10's to 500. Count backwards by 10's from 500.	Draw a birds-eye view of your bedroom.	Find a large number in the newspaper. Cut it out. Read it to your parents.	Design a division problem for your parents. Check their work. Grade it.	Say the months of the year, days of the week and exact time of day.	Find an advertisement section in the newspaper. Make a list of bargains for your parents.
Call a friend. Tell them something nice. Hi!	Make a finger puppet from foil. Use it to teach someone how to multiply or add.	Have a garage sale of all your old toys. How much did you make?	Draw a picture of something inside outside and beside a box.	Watch an insect. Draw it. Keep a record of what it does in 1 day.	Make a gallon of cool ade. Open up a Cool Ade Stand. COOL ADE 5¢	Design the most difficult math problem you can. Give it to your parent to do. Check their work.
Think about some one you hurt. Can you tell them you are sorry? Make them a love card.	Write down the directions to make a peanut butter/jelly sandwich. Give the directions to someone to make one for you.	Make a list of animal names from A to Z	Count to 50 by 3's. Is there any left over? 3	Chew a piece of candy. Count the number of chews it took before it disappeared.	Collect some leaves and weeds. Classify them according to length and the according to shape.	Clean the garage or laundry room.
Write a letter to an older person you know.	Hide a treasure. Make a map for a friend with directions to find the treasure.	Find a small bush. Count the leaves on a branch. Can you estimate the total leaves on the whole bush?				

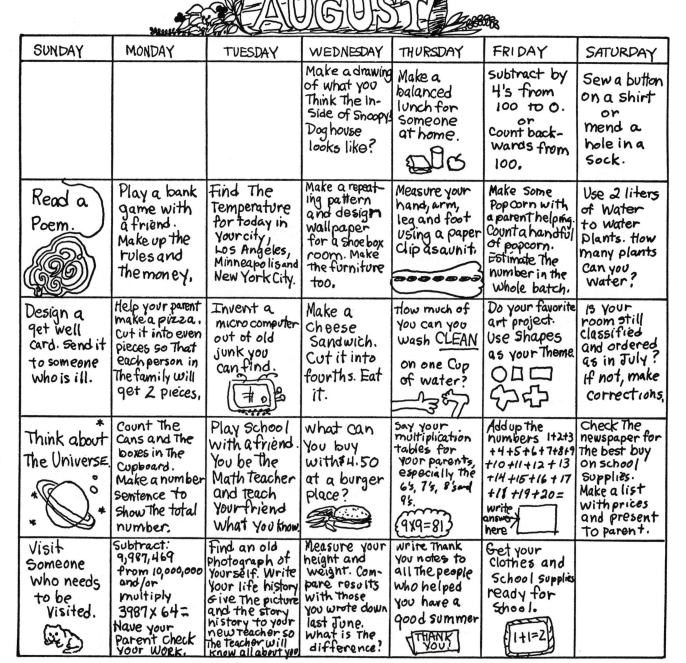

AUGUST

SUNDAY	MONDAY	TUESDAY	WEDNESDAY	THURSDAY	FRIDAY	SATURDAY
			Make a drawing of what you Think The Inside of Snoopy's Dog house looks like?	Make a balanced lunch for someone at home.	Subtract by 4's from 100 to 0. or Count backwards from 100.	Sew a button on a shirt or mend a hole in a sock.
Read a Poem.	Play a bank game with a friend. Make up the rules and the money.	Find The Temperature for today in Your city, Los Angeles, Minneapolis and New York City.	Make a repeating pattern and design wallpaper for a shoe box room. Make the furniture too.	Measure your hand, arm, leg and foot using a paper clip as a unit.	Make some Popcorn with a parent helping. Count a handful of popcorn. Estimate The number in the whole batch.	Use 2 liters of Water to water plants. How many plants can you water?
Design a get well card. Send it to someone who is ill.	Help your parent make a pizza. Cut it into even pieces so That each person in The family will get 2 pieces.	Invent a micro computer out of old junk you can find.	Make a cheese Sandwich. Cut it into fourths. Eat it.	How much of You can you wash CLEAN on one Cup of water?	Do your favorite art project. Use Shapes as your Theme.	Is your room still classified and ordered as in July? If not, make corrections.
Think about The Universe.	Count The cans and The boxes in The Cupboard. Make a number sentence to Show the total number.	Play School with a friend. You be the Math teacher and teach Your friend What you know.	what can you buy with $4.50 at a burger place?	Say your multiplication tables for your parents, especially the 6's, 7's, 8's and 9's. 9x9=81	Add up the numbers 1+2+3 +4+5+6+7+8+9 +10+11+12+13 +14+15+16+17 +18+19+20= write answer here	Check The newspaper for The best buy on school supplies. Make a list with prices and present To parent.
Visit Someone who needs to be Visited.	Subtract: 9,987,469 from 10,000,000 and/or multiply 3987 x 64 = Have your Parent check your work.	Find an old Photograph of Yourself. Write Your life history Give The picture and the story history to your new Teacher so The Teacher will know all about you	Measure your height and weight. Compare results with those you wrote down last June. What is The difference?	Write Thank You notes to all The people who helped You have a good summer THANK YOU!	Get your clothes and School supplies ready for Shool. 1+1=2	

261

APPENDIX

MULTIPLICATION/DIVISION HANDBOOKS
(Includes Directions for Binding)

Materials: Interesting pictures   Magic Markers
Construction paper   Crayons
Glue   Yarn needle
Yarn   Paper hole punch

Procedure:

1. Choose a number from 1 through 9. Factor it.
   Example: 8   0 × 8   8 × 1
                 8 × 0   2 × 4
                 1 × 8   4 × 2

2. Illustrate each factor and make a cover for the book.

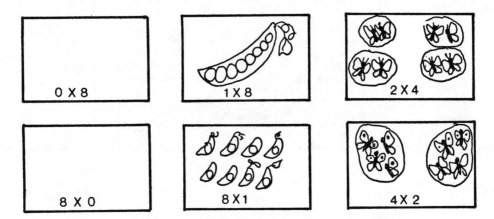

3. Bind the book using a Japanese binding procedure. First, punch holes in each page that has an illustration. The holes should be 1 inch apart. Second, thread a yarn needle with yarn that is approximately 36 inches long. Bind as shown in the figures.

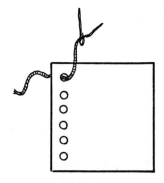

Insert yarn through first hole.

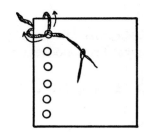

Loop yarn around top of book and again around spine of book.

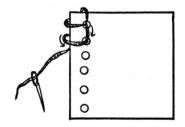

Insert needle into next hole and loop yarn around spine of book. Needle is now on back side.

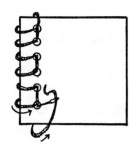

Go to the next hole and loop yarn around. Continue procedure until the last hole is reached.

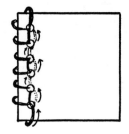

Finish binding by returning to top hole by sewing in and out of the holes. Tie the ends together.

REFERENCES AND SUGGESTED READINGS

References

1. Unit 14, *Exploring Symmetrical Patterns*. Minnesota Mathematics and Science Teaching Project, University of Minnesota, Minneapolis, Minnesota, 1971.

2. Unit 25, *Multiplication and Motion*. Minnesota Mathematics and Science Teaching Project, University of Minnesota, Minneapolis, Minnesota, 1970, pp. 22-24.

Suggested Readings

1. Blackburn, J. and Powell, W.C. *One at a Time All at Once: The Creative Teacher's Guide to Individualized Instruction Without Anarchy*. Santa Monica, CA: Goodyear Pub. Co., 1976.

2. Blake, J. and Ernst, B. *The Great Perpetual Learning Machine*. Boston: Little, Brown and Co., 1976.

3. Blake, J., Ryberg, S., and Sebastian, J. *Bag of Tricks, Instructional Activities and Games*. Denver, CO: Love Publishing Co., 1976.

4. Croft, D. J. and Hess, R. D. *An Activities Handbook for Teachers of Young Children*. Boston: Houghton Mifflin Co., 1980.

5. Forte, I., Pangle, M. A., and Tupa, R. *Center Stuff for Nooks, Crannies and Corners*. Nashville, TN: Incentive Publications, 1973.

6. Krulik, S. and Rudnick, J. *Problem Solving: A Handbook for Teachers*. Boston: Allyn and Bacon, Inc., 1980.

7. Newmann, D. *The Teacher's Desk Companion*. New York: Macmillan Educational Corp., 1977.

8. Sheffield, L. J. *Problem Solving in Math*, Books C, D and E. New York: Scholastic Book Services, 1982.

9. Thiessen, D. and Wild, M. *The Elementary Math Teacher's Handbook: Activities for Teaching Elementary School Mathematics*. New York: John Wiley & Sons, Inc., 1982.

10. Troutman, A. P. and Lichtenberg, B. K. *Mathematics: A Good Beginning*. Monterey, CA: Brooks/Cole Publishing Co., 1982.

11. Wankelman, W. and Wigg, P. *Arts and Crafts: A Handbook of Arts and Crafts for Elementary and Junior High School Teachers*. Dubuque, IA: William C. Brown Co., 1982.

SOME RESOURCES FOR ADDITIONAL PRIMARY MATH ACTIVITIES

Activity Resources Company, Inc.
P.O. Box 4875
Hayward, CA 94540

Creative Teaching Press
P.O. Box P-92
Huntington Beach, CA 92647

Creative Publications
3977 East Bayshore Road
P.O. Box 10328
Palo Alto, CA 94303

Dale Seymour Publications
P.O. Box 10888
Palo Alto, CA 94303

Developmental Learning Materials
1 DLM Park
Allen, TX 75002

Educational Progress Corporation
4235 South Memorial
Tulsa, OK 74145

Educational Teaching Aids
159 West Kinzie Street
Chicago, IL 60610

Humanics Limited
P.O. Box 7447
Atlanta, GA 30309

Incentive Publications
Box 12522
Nashville, TN 37212

Instructor Magazine
757 Third Avenue
New York, NY 10017

Schooldays Magazine
Frank Schaffer Publications, Inc.
1028 Via Mirabel
Palo Verdes Estates, CA 90274

The Wright Group
7620 Miramar Road
Suite 4100
San Diego, CA 92126

SKILLS INDEX

MATHEMATICS

SKILLS	KINDERGARTEN	GRADE 1	GRADE 2	GRADE 3 and Up
ADDITION				
1 through 10	65, 68, 69, 70, 72	65, 68, 69, 70, 72, 73, 74, 78	65, 69, 70, 72, 73, 74, 78	
1 through 20/ with regrouping		75, 76, 79, 80, 81	75, 76, 79, 80, 81	75, 76, 79, 80, 81
one, two, three and four digits		96, 97, 98, 238, 240	96, 97, 98, 238, 240	96, 97, 98, 100, 238, 240
COUNTING BY:				
ones	10, 12, 28, 29, 30, 33, 34	10, 12, 28, 30, 33, 34	10, 29, 30, 33, 34	10
twos	10, 34	10, 34, 35	10, 34, 35	10, 35
fives	10, 34	10, 34, 36, 37	10, 34, 36, 37	10, 36, 37
tens	10, 34	10, 34, 38, 39	10, 34, 38, 39	10, 38, 39
DIVISION			83, 84, 85, 86, 87, 88, 243	83, 84, 85, 86, 87, 88, 243
FRACTIONS				
identifying/recognizing parts		107, 108, 109, 110, 111, 114, 116	107, 108, 109, 110, 111, 112, 114, 115, 116	107, 108, 109, 110, 111, 112, 114, 115, 116, 118, 119
>, <, and =		108	108, 117	108, 117
mixed numerals		108	108	108
addition of		108	108	108
subtraction of		108	108	108
GEOMETRY (see Shapes)				
GRAPHS		250, 251, 252	248, 250, 251, 252	248, 250, 251, 252
MEASUREMENT				
length	125, 126	121, 124, 125, 126, 127	121, 124, 125, 126, 127	121, 124, 125, 126, 127
perimeter		121, 124	121, 124	121, 124
area		124	124	124
weight	129	129	129, 130	129, 130
MULTIPLICATION			82, 84, 85, 86, 87, 88, 243	82, 84, 85, 86, 87, 88, 243
MONEY				
values to 25¢	104	104, 105, 202, 203, 204, 205	202, 203, 204, 205	202, 203, 204, 205
values to 50¢		206, 208	104, 105, 206, 208	104, 105, 206, 208
values to $1.00		209, 210, 212, 213, 214, 215	209, 210, 212, 213, 214, 215	209, 210, 212, 213, 214, 215
NUMERATION				
classifying	4, 7, 8, 10, 235, 236, 237, 246	4, 7, 8, 10, 236, 237, 238, 246	4, 8, 10, 236, 237, 238, 246	4, 8, 10, 236, 237, 238, 246

MATHEMATICS (cont.)

SKILLS	KINDERGARTEN	GRADE 1	GRADE 2	GRADE 3 and Up
negative numbers				57
odd/even numbers		59	59	59
one to one correspondence	41, 43, 44, 47	41, 43, 44, 45, 46, 47	45, 46, 47	46
ordering/sequencing	10, 31, 32, 41, 42, 47, 48, 49, 51, 53, 236, 242	10, 31, 32, 41, 42, 47, 48, 49, 51, 52, 53, 236, 242	10, 31, 32, 47, 48, 49, 51, 52, 76, 236, 242	10, 52, 76, 236
recognizing numerals	31, 32, 41, 42, 43, 47, 53	31, 32, 41, 42, 43, 46, 47, 53	31, 42, 46, 47	46
recognizing number words	46, 47	46, 47	46, 47	46
PATTERNS (see Symmetry)				
PLACE VALUE	104	91, 93, 94, 96, 97, 98, 104, 105, 245	91, 93, 94, 96, 97, 98, 102, 104, 105, 245	91, 93, 94, 96, 97, 98, 100, 102, 104, 105, 245
PROBLEM SOLVING	242, 245, 246, 253	236, 237, 238, 240, 242, 245, 246, 253	236, 237, 238, 240, 242, 245, 246, 253	236, 237, 238, 240, 242, 245, 246, 253
RECOGNIZING/NAMING OPPOSITES				
thick/thin	3, 4	3, 4	4	4
above/below	22, 23	22, 23		
large/small	6, 7	6, 7		
long/short	8, 9. 10	8, 9, 10	8, 9, 10	8, 10
left/right	4, 8, 24, 25	4, 8, 24, 25	4, 8	4, 8
SHAPES/GEOMETRY				
basic shapes	11, 12, 14, 15, 16, 17, 20, 21, 179	11, 12, 14, 15, 17, 20, 21, 179	14, 16, 17, 21, 179	14, 17, 179
grouping shapes	19, 132, 134, 136, 141	19, 132, 134, 136, 140, 141, 142, 153, 158, 159, 161	19, 132, 134, 136, 139, 140, 141, 142, 153, 158, 159, 161, 164, 169	132, 134, 136, 139, 140, 141, 142, 153, 158, 159, 161, 164, 169
polygons		142, 153, 159, 161	142, 153, 159, 161, 164, 169	142, 153, 159, 161, 164, 169
SUBTRACTION				
1 through 10	65	65	65	
1 through 20/with regrouping	240	240	76, 79, 80, 81, 240	76, 79, 80, 81 ,240
one, two, three and four digits		97, 98, 243	97, 98, 102, 243	97, 98, 100, 102, 243
SYMMETRY/PATTERNS				
simple patterns	172	172		
reproducing a pattern	199, 242	199, 242	199, 242	199, 242
turning/rotational patterns	173, 175, 176, 177, 178, 179	173, 175, 176, 177, 178, 179, 181	114, 115, 173, 175, 176, 177, 178, 179, 181, 182	114, 115, 173, 175, 176, 177, 178, 179, 181, 182
repeating/translational patterns	183, 184, 186, 188, 242	183, 184, 186, 188, 242	183, 184, 186, 187, 188, 242	183, 184, 186, 187, 188, 242
reflecting/bilateral patterns	190, 191, 192, 197, 198	190, 191, 192, 195, 197, 198	109, 189, 190, 191, 192, 193, 195, 197, 198	109, 189, 190, 191, 192, 193, 195, 197, 198
TIME				
hours	232	232, 233	232, 233	232, 233
days	220, 225	220, 225	220, 225	220, 225
months	225, 228, 240, 244	225, 228, 230, 240, 244	225, 226, 228, 230, 240, 244	225, 226, 228, 230, 240, 244
morning/noon/night	218, 219	218, 219		

ART

SKILLS/MEDIA	KINDERGARTEN	GRADE 1	GRADE 2	GRADE 3 and Up
CRAFTS	9, 11, 28, 29, 44, 69, 172, 197	9, 11, 28, 29, 36, 38, 44, 69, 110, 139, 172, 197	9, 11, 29, 36, 38, 69, 84, 88, 110, 115, 121, 139, 140, 158, 172, 182, 187, 193, 197	36, 38, 84, 88, 110, 115, 118, 119, 121, 139, 140, 158, 172, 182, 188, 193, 197
CRAYON	4, 21, 22, 47, 132	4, 21, 22, 35, 39, 45, 47, 132	4, 21, 30, 33, 35, 39, 45, 47, 73	4, 35, 39, 85, 132
DESIGNING WITH MIXED MEDIA	134, 158, 173, 199, 220, 253	134, 158, 173, 195, 199, 220, 253	134, 158, 173, 181, 195, 199, 220, 253	134, 158, 173, 181, 195, 199, 220, 253
PAINT	23, 30, 33, 198, 228	23, 30, 33, 73, 74, 198, 228	74, 85, 132, 195, 198, 226, 228	132, 195, 198, 226, 228
PAPER	10, 24, 31, 68, 133, 134, 136, 141, 176, 177, 178, 179, 190	10, 24, 31, 68, 111, 114, 121, 132, 136, 141, 175, 176, 177, 178, 179, 183, 184, 190	10, 31, 111, 114, 121, 132, 136, 141, 175, 176, 177, 178, 179, 183, 184, 189, 190	10, 111, 114, 121, 132, 156, 141, 175, 176, 177, 178, 179, 183, 184, 189, 190
PRINTING	12, 17, 184, 191	12, 17, 52, 78, 127, 136, 184, 186, 191	17, 52, 78, 86, 117, 127, 136, 184, 186, 191	17, 52, 86, 117, 127, 136, 184, 186, 191
SCULPTURE	3, 14, 15, 16, 19, 20, 72, 138, 179, 190, 192, 228	3, 14, 15, 16, 19, 20, 72, 81, 138, 179, 190, 192, 228	14, 16, 19, 72, 75, 79, 81, 138, 159, 179, 190, 192, 228	14, 72, 75, 79, 81, 138, 159, 179, 190, 192, 228

READING/LANGUAGE ARTS

SKILLS	KINDERGARTEN	GRADE 1	GRADE 2	GRADE 3 and Up
ALPHABET RECOGNITION	6	6, 203, 250, 251, 252	203, 248, 250, 251, 252	203, 248, 250, 251, 253
CLASSIFICATION	4, 7, 8, 10, 24, 138, 218, 219, 246	4, 7, 8, 10, 24, 138, 218, 219, 236, 246	4, 8, 10, 138, 219, 236, 246	4, 8, 10, 119, 138, 236, 246
CREATIVE WRITING	28, 35, 220	28, 35, 52, 55, 91, 93, 94, 97, 107, 220, 230	52, 55, 76, 88, 91, 93, 94, 97, 107, 220, 230	52, 55, 76, 88, 91, 93, 97, 107, 119, 220, 230
FOLLOWING DIRECTIONS (see Listening)				
LISTENING	8, 25, 31, 44, 49, 65, 68, 72, 176, 245	8, 25, 31, 38, 44, 45, 49, 59, 65, 68, 72, 74, 176, 245	8, 31, 38, 45, 49, 59, 65, 72, 74, 176, 245	8, 38, 59, 72, 119, 176, 245
SENTENCE PATTERNS	15	15, 110, 116, 230	79, 80, 81, 110, 112, 114, 115, 116, 230	79, 80, 81, 110, 112, 114, 115, 116, 118, 230
SEQUENCING	10, 31, 32, 47, 53, 125, 172, 188	10, 31, 32, 47, 53, 125, 172, 188	10, 31, 32, 47, 125	10, 125
SPELLING	220	202, 220	202, 220	202, 220
VISUAL DISCRIMINATION	6, 31, 32, 48	6, 31, 42, 46, 48, 107	31, 32, 46, 107	46, 107
WORD RECOGNITION	46, 47, 108	46, 47, 108, 109, 114	46, 47, 108, 109, 114	46, 47, 108, 109, 114, 118